POWER
THOUGHTS
DEVOTIONAL

POWER
THOUGHTS
DEVOTIONAL

365 DAILY INSPIRATIONS FOR
WINNING THE
BATTLE OF THE MIND

JOYCE MEYER

FaithWords

NEW YORK   BOSTON   NASHVILLE

Unless otherwise noted, Scriptures are taken from *The Amplified Bible* (AMP). *The Amplified Bible*, copyright © 1965, 1987 by The Zondervan Corporation. *The Amplified New Testament* copyright © 1954, 1958, 1987 by The Lockman Foundation. Used by permission.

Scripture quotations marked (KJV) are taken from the King James Version of the Bible.

Scripture quotations marked (NASB) are taken from the *New American Standard Bible*®. Copyright © 1960, 1962, 1963, 1968, 1971, 1972, 1973, 1975, 1977, 1995 by The Lockman Foundation. Used by permission.

Scripture quotations marked (NIV) are taken from the *Holy Bible: New International Version*®. Copyright © 1973, 1978, 1984 by International Bible Society. Used by permission of Zondervan Publishing House. All rights reserved.

Scripture quotations marked *The Message* are taken from *The Message*. Copyright © 1993, 1994, 1995, 1996, 2000, 2001, 2002. Used by permission of NavPress Publishing Group.

Scripture quotations marked (NKJV) are taken from the *New King James Version*. Copyright © 1979, 1980, 1982 by Thomas Nelson, Inc., Publishers.

Scripture quotations marked (NLT) are taken from the *Holy Bible*, New Living Translation. Copyright © 1996. Used by permission of Tyndale House Publishers, Inc., Wheaton, Illinois 60189. All rights reserved.

FaithWords
Hachette Book Group
237 Park Avenue
New York, NY 10017

www.faithwords.com

Printed in the United States of America

RRD-C

First Edition: October 2013

10 9 8 7 6 5 4 3 2 1

FaithWords is a division of Hachette Book Group, Inc.
The FaithWords name and logo are trademarks of Hachette Book Group, Inc.

The Hachette Speakers Bureau provides a wide range of authors for speaking events. To find out more, go to www.hachettespeakersbureau.com or call (866) 376-6591.

The publisher is not responsible for websites (or their content) that are not owned by the publisher.

Library of Congress Control Number: 2013941780

ISBN: 978-1-4555-1744-2

POWER
THOUGHTS
DEVOTIONAL

Introduction

Many years ago, I was extremely negative. My thoughts were all negative, so the words of my mouth were negative, and therefore my life was negative. When I really began to study the Word and to trust God to restore me, one of the first things I realized was that the negativity had to go.

When I began eliminating the negativity in my life, I was initially frustrated because I didn't see change. That's when God spoke to my heart: "Joyce, you have stopped saying negative things, but you have not started saying positive things."

It wasn't easy, but God taught me that I can *choose* my thoughts and control the way I think and speak. I don't have to just think any old thing that falls into my head. I can think things on purpose that will positively affect my life. I can think in line with God's Word and speak it as my daily confession. I can overcome negative thinking by setting my mind and keeping it set on things above. And you can too.

I have probably never written a book that did not include some teaching about the power of words and the power of the mind, and

I probably never will. That is how important this subject is, and I want you to take it seriously. I want you to think and speak on purpose daily!

Galatians 6:7 says we reap what we sow. Therefore, if you think positive thoughts and speak them aloud as your confession, you will reap positive rewards in your life. I don't mean you'll never have a situation in your life that you don't like, but you can learn to look for the positive in all circumstances and be grateful for what you do have, trusting God to care for you and work all things together for good (see Romans 8:28). You can think and speak: "I believe God is working, and I will see the results in my life!"

Like my book *Power Thoughts*, this devotional isn't meant to just be read; it's meant to be used. I encourage you to take time each morning to read the daily Scripture and devotional and commit the power thought to memory. Then take it to the next level and make it part of your confession. It is important to take time first thing in the morning to fill your mind with positive, Scripture-based power thoughts you can think and speak throughout your day so you are ready when the negative thoughts and circumstances come your way. It can be especially helpful when you find yourself speaking negatively to replace those words with your daily power thought. I truly believe if you make these power thoughts part of your life and belief system—which you can do by thinking and speaking them *daily*—you will see a dramatic change in your life.

From the very beginning of your day, before you've even gotten out of bed, choose your thoughts and words carefully. They will set the tone for your entire day. Meditate on the power thought at the end of each devotional throughout your day, and you will begin to think, speak, act, and even feel more positive as you choose to enjoy your everyday life!

Make the choice: renew your mind and mouth by thinking and speaking power thoughts daily.

> *Because if you acknowledge and confess with your lips that*
> *Jesus is Lord and in your heart believe (adhere to, trust in,*
> *and rely on the truth) that God raised Him from the dead, you*
> *will be saved. For with the heart a person believes (adheres*
> *to, trusts in, and relies on Christ) and so is justified (declared*
> *righteous, acceptable to God), and with the mouth he confesses*
> *(declares openly and speaks out freely his faith) and confirms*
> *[his] salvation.*   ROMANS 10:9–10

Mind, Mouth, Moods, and Attitudes

Behold, I give unto you power to tread on serpents and
scorpions, and over all the power of the enemy: and nothing
shall by any means hurt you.   LUKE 10:19 KJV

This is typically how your mind, mouth, moods, and attitudes are connected: When you have a negative circumstance, you have a negative thought. Then you say a negative thing about the circumstance, and then your mood begins to sink. Next you get a bad attitude, and you end up with more negative circumstances than you started with.

But you can break this cycle in your life. Did you know that? Luke 10:19 says we have power to "tread on serpents and scorpions, and over all the power of the enemy" (KJV). To *tread* means "to walk all over, to take steps, to take action, to resist." You have the power to do these things. When you have a problem, nothing negative will fix it. Keep your mind, mouth, moods, and attitudes positive, and watch God work miracles on your behalf.

———

Power Thought: In Christ, I have power over negative thinking.

Cast Your Care

Casting the whole of your care [all your anxieties, all your
worries, all your concerns, once and for all] on Him, for He
cares for you affectionately and cares about you watchfully.

1 PETER 5:7

You can pray about everything and worry about nothing. When
you worry, it says you think you can solve your own problems
better than God can. But you were not built to handle problems
in your own strength. You were created by God to be dependent
upon Him; so bring Him your challenges in life and allow Him to
help you with them.

Can you imagine your life without worry? Why not start today
to live a worry-free life? Ask the Lord to show you every time you
are taking on care instead of casting it off. When He makes you
aware of it, be willing to immediately cast it on Him—you will
enjoy life so much more. After a period of time, you will actually
find it difficult to worry! It just won't suit you any longer.

Power Thought: I can cast my care on God because He
cares for me.

I Am and I Can

And we know that all things work together for good to them that
love God, to them who are the called according to his purpose.
ROMANS 8:28 KJV

You need to have an "I am" and an "I can" attitude. Fill your
thoughts and your words with these confessions daily, and then
you will bring more joy into your life!

- I am a new creation in Christ (see 2 Corinthians 5:17).
- I can live in perfect peace (see Isaiah 26:3).
- I am slow to speak, quick to hear, and slow to anger (see James 1:19).
- I can do all things through Christ, Who strengthens me (see Philippians 4:13).
- I am more than a conqueror in Christ (see Romans 8:37).
- I can have the mind of Christ (see 1 Corinthians 2:16).
- I am dead to sin and alive to righteousness (see Romans 6:11).
- I can overcome evil with good (see Romans 12:21).

Power Thought: All efforts to train my mind and my
mouth to think and speak more like God work together to
achieve God's purpose for my life.

It Is Time for Change

For My yoke is wholesome (useful, good—not harsh, hard, sharp, or pressing, but comfortable, gracious, and pleasant), and My burden is light and easy to be borne.

MATTHEW 11:30

When what you are doing doesn't give you joy anymore, that is a strong indication God is finished with whatever He was working through you to do. When you start to think, *I'm laboring with this now. It doesn't minister to me anymore,* don't complain, blame, or continue until you end up burned-out. Have the boldness and courage to say, "I did things a certain way for a long time, but I believe God is leading me to do something else."

Life is easy and full of joy when you depend on God and His leading. Pray for God to lead you to where He wants you to be— even if that means embracing change.

Power Thought: I am not afraid of change because it leads me to new beginnings.

Bridle Your Tongue

For we all often stumble and fall and offend in many things.
And if anyone does not offend in speech [never says the wrong
things], he is a fully developed character and a perfect man,
able to control his whole body and to curb his entire nature.

JAMES 3:2

According to this Scripture, the one thing proving our level of spiritual maturity isn't how religious we are—whether we can quote Scripture, or the good works we do—it is the words from our mouths.

James 1:26 says, "If anyone thinks himself to be religious (piously observant of the external duties of his faith) and does not *bridle his tongue* but deludes his own heart, this person's religious service is worthless (futile, barren)" (emphasis added).

No matter how religious you think you are, the true test proving your spirituality is whether you bridle your tongue or not. *Bridle* means "to restrain or control." If we aren't controlling our tongues, we are not operating in the level of maturity God wants us to have.

Power Thought: I am able to control the words I speak by God's grace.

Attitude Is Everything

He [can be trusted] not to let you be tempted and tried and assayed beyond your ability and strength of resistance and power to endure, but with the temptation He will [always] also provide the way out (the means of escape to a landing place), that you may be capable and strong and powerful to bear up under it patiently.   1 CORINTHIANS 10:13

Some of the challenges we face in life may be very difficult ones, but God never allows more to come upon us than we can bear. In fact, with every temptation, He always provides a way out. The Scripture above not only says He provides a way out, but it also says He gives us the strength to bear up under trials with patience. That means we can go through them with a good attitude! Maintaining a good attitude in the midst of something unpleasant is the key to victory, and it enables us to enjoy the journey.

———————————

Power Thought: I can maintain a good attitude during trials, knowing that God provides my way out.

The Joy of the Lord

Be not grieved and depressed, for the joy of the Lord is your
strength and stronghold.   NEHEMIAH 8:10

Joy is closely connected to our expectations (what we think and believe). In other words, the more you *expect* good things to happen to you, the more joy you will have. What are you expecting right now? If you're expecting nothing, that is probably what you will get.

Don't look to the world to form your hopes, dreams, and expectations, because even if you get them, they won't be fulfilling. Look to God, Who is able to do exceedingly, abundantly, above and beyond anything you could possibly imagine (see Ephesians 3:20).

Expect Him to do great things in your life, not because you deserve it, but because He is good!

Power Thought: I am expecting God to do amazingly good things in my life.

Step Out in Faith

And Peter answered Him, Lord, if it is You, command me to come to You on the water. He said, Come! So Peter got out of the boat and walked on the water, and he came toward Jesus.

MATTHEW 14:28–29

When Peter got out of the boat, his action proved that he had faith in God's word when he heard Jesus say, "Come." Is God asking you to do something and you're waiting to *feel safe*? If so, that isn't faith. In order to do or have greater things, we are usually required to let go of what we have and head into the unknown.

God told Abraham to leave his country, his home, and his relatives and go to a land that He would show him how to get to *after* he started the journey. Abraham had to leave, not knowing where he was going; now *that* is faith!

As you take steps of faith to be obedient to God, you will experience His faithfulness, and your faith will become strong. Don't let fear stop you because God will never leave you or forsake you.

Power Thought: I am not afraid to take a step of faith.

The Touch of God

I will give them one heart [a new heart] and I will put a new
spirit within them; and I will take the stony [unnaturally
hardened] heart out of their flesh, and will give them a heart of
flesh [sensitive and responsive to the touch of their God].

EZEKIEL 11:19

God has made us sensitive to His touch and wants to lead us to
do things that are good for us, like spending time with Him, but
He doesn't want us to turn our devotional time into a law—like
believing we *have* to pray for fifteen minutes, read the Word for
twenty minutes, and confess the Word for ten minutes each day in
order to please Him.

As soon as we view things as laws and rules, the joy is drained
out of them and they are turned into works of the flesh. Let God
lead you in your time spent with Him, and you will never get
bored. The Holy Spirit is creative, and He will help you keep your
time with God fresh and exciting.

Before we accepted Christ, we were too hard-hearted to be led
by the Spirit, but God has given us new hearts, and we can follow
His guidance.

Power Thought: I am obedient to the touch of God that is
guiding and directing my life.

Determine Your Priorities

You shall have no other gods before or besides Me.

EXODUS 20:3

The best way to determine if God is first in your life is to slow down and ask yourself some simple questions: *What do I think about the most? What do I pray and talk about the most? What do I do with my time?*

You see, we always make time for what we really want to do—no matter how busy we are. If you want to spend time with God, then you are going to make Him a priority.

Ask the Holy Spirit to show you where your priorities are out of line. Then allow His conviction to motivate you to seek a deeper relationship with God. It is God, through the power of the Holy Spirit, Who will give you the ability to adjust your lifestyle and bring it in line with the Word (see 1 Thessalonians 5:23 NLT). If you truly want Him to, He will enable you to put God first in your thoughts, conversations, and actions. You may need to make some changes in your schedule, but they will be ones that will produce good results.

Power Thought: God is number one in my life.

The Breastplate of Integrity

*Stand therefore [hold your ground], having tightened the belt
of truth around your loins and having put on the breastplate of
integrity and of moral rectitude and right standing with God.*

EPHESIANS 6:14

Integrity is vitally important to our walk with God. People with
integrity take responsibility for their actions. They keep their commitments instead of making excuses for not keeping them. They
do what they tell people they are going to do, and, if for some reason they absolutely cannot, then they contact the person, give an
explanation (not an excuse), and ask to be released from the commitment. We expect God to keep His promises, and He expects us
to keep ours.

If people truly understood what the word *integrity* means, we
would hopefully have more people in the world with good character, trying to keep their integrity. Since God has given us the
"breastplate of integrity," we know we are to do battle against the
enemy of deceit. Let us all choose to do right and trust God to
honor our decisions.

Power Thought: I am committed to living a life of
integrity; I always keep my word.

Abiding in the Word

*If you live in Me [abide vitally united to Me] and My words
remain in you and continue to live in your hearts, ask whatever
you will, and it shall be done for you.*   JOHN 15:7

Most Christians know the importance of reading the Bible, but
many do not understand the importance of abiding (living and
remaining, holding fast and continuing) in the Word and allowing
the Word to abide in them.

When we diligently study the Word and keep Scripture verses
in our hearts, we have instant access to them whenever we need
them, and Jesus promised we can ask for whatever we need in
prayer and receive it.

Abiding in the Word and allowing the Word to abide in us
makes us true disciples of Jesus (see John 8:31). It gives us more
power in our prayer lives, and having power in prayer gives us
power over the enemy.

Power Thought: The power of God is available to me
when I abide in God's Word.

Show No Mercy

*And when the Lord your God gives them over to you and you
smite them, then you must utterly destroy them. You shall make
no covenant with them, or show mercy to them.*

DEUTERONOMY 7:2

Negative thoughts and words are our enemies because they hinder
us from being the people we want to be. When enemies are trying to destroy you—even when it is through your own negative
thoughts and words—you cannot show them mercy; you have to
resist them in the power of the Holy Spirit.

In Deuteronomy 7:1–2, God was leading the Israelites to possess the land He had promised them, just as He is leading us into
the good life He has promised us. There were many enemy nations
coming against them, just as the devil is against us. God told the
Israelites to "utterly destroy" the ungodly enemy nations and to
"make no covenant with them, or show mercy to them," and we
must do the same thing with the ungodly thoughts, words, and
actions we have that are stealing our destinies. Be firm, steadfast,
and resist the devil at his onset (see 1 Peter 5:8–9).

Power Thought: I show no mercy to those things that try
to steal the quality of life Jesus has for me.

Spiritual Disciplines

For the time being no discipline brings joy, but seems grievous and painful; but afterwards it yields a peaceable fruit of righteousness to those who have been trained by it [a harvest of fruit which consists in righteousness—in conformity to God's will in purpose, thought, and action, resulting in right living and right standing with God].   HEBREWS 12:11

Just as we need natural disciplines in our lives, such as the discipline to work, disciplines concerning appetites, finances, and so on, we also need spiritual disciplines, such as prayer, Bible study, and confessing God's Word out loud.

As we discipline ourselves to do these things, they will become habits. Then we will see good results just as we see good results from any other discipline applied over a period of time. Discipline doesn't produce immediate joy, but it is an investment that will pay great dividends in due time. Discipline is wisdom because a wise person always does now what he or she will be satisfied with later on in life.

Power Thought: I discipline myself in all areas of life because it is wise to do so.

Pray and Say God's Word

Fear not [there is nothing to fear], for I am with you; do not look around you in terror and be dismayed, for I am your God.

ISAIAH 41:10

We must accept the fact that fear is a human emotion—we all experience it to some degree, but we also know we can live boldly and courageously because God has told us He is always with us. And because of that, we can choose to not live according to the fear we feel.

God taught me to use what I call the "power twins" to help me defeat the spirit of fear. They are "I pray" and "I say." When I feel fear, I begin to *pray* and ask for God's help, then I *say*, "I will not fear!" Use these power twins as soon as you feel fearful about anything, and you will be able to keep fear from controlling you. We can learn to manage the emotion of fear and not let it manage us.

Power Thought: I will not live in fear.

Live Love

We know that we have passed over out of death into Life by the
fact that we love the brethren (our fellow Christians). He who
does not love abides (remains, is held and kept continually) in
[spiritual] death.   1 JOHN 3:14

From start to finish, in all kinds of ways, God's Word encourages
and challenges us to love other people; it is the example Jesus set
for us throughout His life and ministry on Earth.

If you truly desire to love others the way God loves you, you
must first purpose to fill your mind with kind, loving, unselfish,
and generous thoughts. Take a few minutes each morning and ask
God to show you what you can do for somebody else that day. You
can even choose a specific person. Focus on loving others, and
you'll have a life full of love and happiness and be a great encourager to others.

Power Thought: My life is worth living because I live to
love others.

The Written Word of God

Blessed (happy, fortunate, to be envied) are they who keep His testimonies, and who seek, inquire for and of Him and crave Him with the whole heart.   PSALM 119:2

In order to know God—what to expect from Him and what He expects from you—you must know His Word. It's not possible for God to say one thing but do another. He cannot lie, and He's always faithful to perform what He has promised.

I know many people who have studied God's Word diligently and whose lives have been changed, but I also know many who, although they would like their lives to improve, won't discipline themselves to study and learn the Word or to speak the Word. Spending time with God by studying the Word is your choice, and only you can make it. When you make that choice to seek Him with your whole heart, it won't take long before the desire to really know God and His Word becomes a natural response.

Power Thought: I crave God with my whole heart and seek Him through His Word.

Are God's Thoughts Your Thoughts?

*For My thoughts are not your thoughts, neither are your ways
My ways, says the Lord.*   ISAIAH 55:8

Whose thoughts are you thinking? If your thoughts are not God's thoughts, I recommend changing your thinking! If we want to have what God wants us to have, then we will need to learn to think the way He thinks.

In Jeremiah 29:11, God says, "For I know the thoughts that I think toward you" (KJV). God has thoughts for you. Do you think about you and your life the way God is thinking about you?

If you're not thinking the way God is thinking, you are not going to end up with God's plan for you. The Bible says in Proverbs 23:7, "For as he thinks in his heart, so is he." You can stop God's plan by thinking your own fleshly thoughts, or agreeing with others' or the devil's thoughts, or you can think God's thoughts and believe and receive the good plan He has for your life. Who are you in agreement with?

Power Thought: What God believes about me, I also believe.

It's Your Future

Therefore I always exercise and discipline myself [mortifying my body, deadening my carnal affections, bodily appetites, and worldly desires, endeavoring in all respects] to have a clear (unshaken, blameless) conscience, void of offense toward God and toward men.   ACTS 24:16

The Roman poet Horace wrote: "Rule your mind or it will rule you." The enemy wants your mind; he wants to control or influence as much of your thinking as possible, but you do not have to let him. The key to overcoming him is learning to discipline your thinking, and disciplining yourself *to believe* you are disciplined is the beginning. As my son once said, "Discipline is a discipline!"

Most people don't get excited when the subject of discipline comes up. However, if you learn to understand the power, the liberty, the joy, and the victory discipline brings to your life, you will embrace it eagerly.

———————————

Power Thought: Disciplining my mind now will reap the results I want in my future.

Acknowledge God

*In all your ways know, recognize, and acknowledge Him, and
He will direct and make straight and plain your paths.*

PROVERBS 3:6

It is so easy to start making a plan instead of waiting on God to
give us His plan. Sometimes we are so entrenched in our own plans
that we don't even sense the leading of the Holy Spirit. But the
proverb says to acknowledge God in *all* our ways, and that means
to care about what He thinks and submit our plans to Him for
approval.

Having a plan is not a bad thing, but we can simply say to God
each day, "Lord, I have a plan for today, but I acknowledge You in
it. And if You don't approve of any part of it, then I am willing to
change and do what You want." If you truly care about what God
desires, He will direct you in the way you should go if any changes
need to be made to your plans.

Power Thought: I acknowledge God in *all* my plans, and
He always guides me.

Let Your Words Be Positive and Few

*You heard Me tell you, I am going away and I am coming
[back] to you. If you [really] loved Me, you would have been
glad, because I am going to the Father; for the Father is greater
and mightier than I am.*   JOHN 14:28

Jesus experienced adverse circumstances all the time, and while
He did talk about His situations, He never did so in a negative way.
In the book of John, He told His disciples He was going away, but
they should be happy for Him because it was the will of God. He
went on to say He wouldn't be talking much more with them (see
John 14:28–31).

Jesus knew when to talk, when not to talk, and how to talk. He
obviously knew the power and impact of words. I believe choosing
to say fewer words and making sure the ones He did say were the
right ones helped Him complete God's perfect plan for Him.

Power Thought: When I speak about my situations, I
speak positively.

Right Action Follows Right Thinking

*Strip yourselves of your former nature [put off and discard your
old unrenewed self] . . . and be constantly renewed in the spirit
of your mind [having a fresh mental and spiritual attitude],
and put on the new nature (the regenerate self) created in
God's image, [Godlike] in true righteousness and holiness.*

EPHESIANS 4:22–24

In God's order of things, right thinking comes first, then right
action follows. I like to use Ephesians 4:22–24 when teaching on
this principle. Verse 22 basically tells us to stop acting improperly, and verse 24 tells us to begin acting properly. But verse 23 is
what I call "the bridge Scripture." It tells us how to get from verse
22 (acting improperly) to verse 24 (acting properly): "And be constantly renewed in the spirit of your mind [having a fresh mental
and spiritual attitude]." It is impossible to get from wrong behavior to right behavior without first changing your thoughts to line
up with God's Word and will.

Think about how you can change with God's help, and soon
you will start seeing those changes come to pass.

Power Thought: I constantly renew my mind with God's
Word.

God Will Meet Your Needs

*And why worry about your clothing? Look at the lilies of
the field and how they grow. They don't work or make their
clothing. . . . And if God cares so wonderfully for wildflowers
that are here today and thrown into the fire tomorrow, he will
certainly care for you. Why do you have so little faith?*

MATTHEW 6:28, 30 NLT

Some people feel needy because their families have hurt them or
let them down; others feel needy because of personal experiences
in which they suffered loss. All these circumstances and others
cause people to fear that they may be abandoned in their time of
need. But God doesn't want us to live in fear of losing what we
have or being without what we need. Let us trust God to always
meet all of our needs and to never abandon us. We should compliment Him by believing He is good and by expecting Him to meet
our needs according to the promises in His Word.

Power Thought: I trust God to care for all my needs.

Setting the Tone for Your Day

In the morning You hear my voice, O Lord; in the morning I prepare [a prayer, a sacrifice] for You and watch and wait [for You to speak to my heart].   PSALM 5:3

What was the first thing you said after getting up this morning? I believe we can prophesy (speak forth) and set the tone of the day by what we say at the beginning of it.

Maybe you said, "I'm tired, and I dread going to work." Those kinds of words often come naturally, but you can decide to live supernaturally. You can talk as God would and say what He would say. Can you honestly imagine God saying, "I'm afraid this is going to be a lousy day"? Of course not! He would say something awesome and positive, and we should too—"I have favor everywhere I go"; "Today is going to be an awesome day"; "I'm going to see the hand of God at work today!"

Power Thought: I begin my day with an attitude of praise—praying and listening for God's voice.

The Temptation to Quit

And when He came to the place, He said to them, Pray that you may not [at all] enter into temptation.   LUKE 22:40

Jesus told the disciples twice in one day to pray they wouldn't enter into temptation: "And when He came to the place, He said to them, Pray that you may not [at all] enter into temptation....And when He got up from prayer, He came to the disciples and found them sleeping from grief, and He said to them, Why do you sleep? Get up and pray that you may not enter [at all] into temptation" (Luke 22:40, 45–46).

The best way to resist the temptation to give up when times are hard is to pray that you won't give in to the temptation. It's wiser and more effective to pray and ask for God's help as you stand against temptation than to try to exert willpower alone. Work with God, and pray you won't surrender to the temptation to give up.

Power Thought: I believe God will strengthen me against the temptation to quit.

Speak It, Believe It, Receive It

Wait and hope for and expect the Lord; be brave and of good
courage and let your heart be stout and enduring. Yes, wait for
and hope for and expect the Lord.   PSALM 27:14

I look at words as a way to reach into the spiritual realm and bring those words into reality. For example, if a person continually says, "I am afraid I will lose my job," that person may behave in a way that will cause an employer not to want to keep him or her at the company. Negative words make us feel negative about ourselves, and then we behave in a way that causes others to feel the same way we do.

Thankfully, we can speak positive, life-filled words and see a positive result. For example, if a person continually says, "God wants to bless me and see me enjoy the best life possible," that person will see the favor of God released in his or her life. If we say a thing often enough, silently in our hearts or verbally, we will believe it. The Bible teaches us that we receive what we believe; all of God's promises are received by believing in them. Actually, *believe* means "to receive," and *receive* means "to believe." Believing and receiving cannot be separated. What we believe becomes our reality!

Power Thought: I believe God and trust Him to answer my prayers.

Earthly Blessings

Beloved, I pray that you may prosper in every way and [that your body] may keep well, even as [I know] your soul keeps well and prospers.   3 JOHN 2

In plain, everyday language, this Scripture could read, "My dearly beloved children, I want you to have every earthly blessing you could possibly imagine, but only to the degree that you have spiritual maturity and Christlike character." When you look at the Scripture this way, you get the message, "I need to grow up!"

You don't need to talk God into blessing you. He *wants* to bless you. In fact, He wants to bless you more than you can imagine being blessed (see Ephesians 3:20). But even more than He wants you to *have* something, He wants you to *be* something. He wants you to be Christlike. Once you *are* something—spiritually mature—you will be able to handle *having* the earthly blessings He desires for you and use them for His glory.

Power Thought: God wants me to enjoy every blessing He has in store for my life.

And God Said . . . And It Was So

And God said, Let us make man in our image. . . . So God created man in his own image.

GENESIS 1:26–27 KJV

According to Genesis, God created everything we see with words! He called them into being:

"And God said, Let there be light; and there was light. . . .

"And God said, Let there be a firmament [the expanse of the sky] in the midst of the waters, and let it separate the waters [below] from the waters [above]. . . .

"And God said, Let the waters under the heavens be collected into one place [of standing], and let the dry land appear. And it was so" (Genesis 1:3, 6, 9).

Everything God said came to pass, and you are created in God's image, and your words also have power. Your words can call things into being, so use them wisely! Speak in agreement with and believe in God's plan for your life, and you will see it come to pass.

Power Thought: My words have the power to create my reality.

Discernment Comes from Within

Tune your ears to wisdom, and concentrate on understanding.
PROVERBS 2:2 NLT

Not everything God asks us to do is going to make sense in our minds. Learn how to go with what you sense *inside your heart*. If you don't have peace about doing something, then don't do it. If you have peace about something, don't let your friends talk you out of it just because they don't understand. Even if you are the only one responding your way, be bold enough to follow your heart.

Stop trying to figure things out; just do what God tells you and you will avoid a lot of confusion. Every time you get confused you can think, *I don't know what's going on, and I am not going to try to figure it out. I just want to follow God.* The apostle Paul was a very educated man, and even he came to the point where he said he was determined to know nothing but Christ (see 1 Corinthians 2:2).

Power Thought: I am tuned in to godly wisdom; therefore, I can trust what I sense inside.

Forgive and Forget

[Love] keeps no record of being wronged.

1 CORINTHIANS 13:5 NLT

Most of us are guilty of keeping up-to-date records of all the offenses we have suffered, no matter how big or how small. But if we want joy to operate in our lives, we will have to learn how to forgive *and* forget.

Forgetting is a choice. It's not that we are *unable* to remember, but we *choose* to remember the better things in life: "If there is any virtue and excellence, if there is anything worthy of praise, think on and weigh and take account of these things [fix your minds on them]" (Philippians 4:8). God is telling you the things that will bring you joy. Nowhere does He say to remember what people have done to hurt your feelings or how they have been rude to you or how they did something you didn't want them to do. God wants you to forgive and forget and fill your mind with worthy things.

Power Thought: I am quick to forgive *and* forget; I keep no record of wrongs done to me.

Take Your Thoughts Captive

[Inasmuch as we] refute arguments and theories and
reasonings and every proud and lofty thing that sets itself up
against the [true] knowledge of God; and we lead every thought
and purpose away captive into the obedience of Christ (the
Messiah, the Anointed One) ...

2 CORINTHIANS 10:5

Take captive every thought coming into your mind that does not agree with the Word of God. Lead those thoughts away, and let them be replaced with ones that are obedient to Jesus Christ. In other words, change your mind!

This is something we have to be persistent in doing; and if you feel weary in the beginning of this new endeavor, I understand because I felt the same way. Instead of fighting with negative thoughts, simply replace them with positive ones. If you choose to think something good, then the bad thing cannot occupy that space in your mind anymore. We always overcome evil with good (see Romans 12:21).

Power Thought: My thoughts are obedient to Christ.

Believe in Something

And the Lord answered me and said, Write the vision and engrave it so plainly upon tablets that everyone who passes may [be able to] read [it easily and quickly] as he hastens by.

HABAKKUK 2:2

Begin to believe in something for your life. I always say, "I'd rather believe for a lot and get a little of it than believe for nothing and get all of it." The devil wants you to believe for nothing so he can give it all to you, but God wants you to believe for something.

God wants us to make progress. Begin to dream on purpose. Habakkuk tells us to write down the vision and write it down so plainly that anyone who passes by can see it. Write some things down on paper that you are trusting God to do in your life. Be filled with hope, and be a person of purpose. Study the promises of God and tell Him that you are expecting to see them come to pass in your life.

Power Thought: I have a vision of God's good plan for my life.

Christ's Personal Representatives

So we are Christ's ambassadors, God making His appeal as it
were through us. We [as Christ's personal representatives] beg
you for His sake to lay hold of the divine favor [now offered you]
and be reconciled to God.   2 CORINTHIANS 5:20

We all need a strong foundation of good, solid doctrine. But along
with doctrine, we also need to know how to live our lives. If we
are going to represent Jesus properly, we need to walk victoriously.

The Bible states that we are more than conquerors (see Romans
8:37), and we are to reign as kings in life through Jesus Christ (see
Romans 5:17). When we are victorious, others see it and want the
same victories in their lives. To put it plainly, if we want other people to accept Jesus, we must show them that having a relationship
with Him makes a real difference in our lives. We are His personal
representatives on Earth, and we need to represent Him well.

Power Thought: I am Christ's personal representative; I
will represent Him well, by His grace.

An Everything-Nothing Attitude

Humble yourselves therefore under the mighty hand of God,
that he may exalt you in due time.

1 PETER 5:6 KJV

We shouldn't have high-minded ideas about ourselves, elevating ourselves above others, but we shouldn't be low-minded either. Here is the mind-set I think we ought to have—I call it an "everything-nothing" attitude: *I'm everything with Christ; I'm nothing without Him. I'm no better than you; I'm no worse than you. I'm not above you; I'm not beneath you.*

In 1 Corinthians 15:10, Paul demonstrates the "everything-nothing" attitude: "But by the grace (the unmerited favor and blessing) of God I am what I am." He then says, "I took His grace and I worked really hard, but oh, by the way, even the work you saw me do wasn't really me, it was God manifesting Himself through me" (paraphrase mine).

A prideful person tries to exalt himself, but a humble person exalts God and lets God exalt him in due time.

Power Thought: I humble myself, and God delivers me.

Accountability

Now we know that whatever the Law says, it speaks to those who are under the Law, so that [the murmurs and excuses of] every mouth may be hushed and all the world may be held accountable to God.   ROMANS 3:19

Do you ever say, "I know I shouldn't do this, but..."; "I know I shouldn't say this, but..."; "I know I shouldn't act like this, but..."; "I know I should forgive her, but..."? What we're really saying is, "I know I'm making a wrong choice, but I hope I can get by with it."

We live in a society where many people do not want to be accountable. A lot of people want to be able to make wrong choices and not have wrong results. But it doesn't work that way. *Accountable* means "answerable." Sooner or later we will have to answer for our choices. If we don't choose to be accountable, eventually our circumstances will force us to be accountable.

Power Thought: I make right choices so I will have a right result.

Fight the Good Fight

*Resist the devil [stand firm against him], and he will flee
from you.*
                                                    JAMES 4:7

We can't just hope we will think good thoughts. We have to
actively seek them. We have to think purposely, not passively.

A passive mind is a dangerous thing; passive people want good
things to happen to them, but they just wait around to see what
will happen. They do nothing to contribute to a positive result in
their lives.

The devil wants us to be passive because then he can work his
plan without any opposition from us. But the Bible tells us to resist
the devil, and he will flee. Be an active person who is always working with God toward the result that you desire to see in your life.

Power Thought: I actively resist the devil as I fight the
good fight of faith.

Never Say "No Way"

Jesus said to him, I am the Way and the Truth and the Life;
no one comes to the Father except by (through) Me.

JOHN 14:6

Have you ever faced a situation and said, "There is no way"?
Maybe some of these thoughts weigh on your mind:

There is no way I can handle the pressure at work.

There is no way I can pay my bills at the end of the month.

There is no way I can save my marriage.

There is no way I can keep my house clean and straight.

There is no way I can lose the weight I need to lose.

There is *always* a way. It may not be easy, it may not be convenient, it may not come quickly; but if you will simply keep on
keeping on and refuse to give up, you *will* find a way. Jesus is the
Way, and He will help you find a way where there doesn't seem to
be one.

Power Thought: I refuse to say "no way"; Jesus is the
Way.

Guilt and Forgiveness

*I acknowledged my sin to You, and my iniquity I did not hide.
I said, I will confess my transgressions to the Lord [continually
unfolding the past till all is told]—then You [instantly] forgave
me the guilt and iniquity of my sin. Selah [pause, and calmly
think of that]!*
PSALM 32:5

Jesus forgave all of our sins when He died on the cross, and He
paid the price for our guilt as well. When we acknowledge or
admit our sin to God, telling Him everything, refusing to hide our
sin, we are able to receive His gift of grace. Confession is good for
the soul; it allows us to let go of heavy burdens that are caused by
guilty secrets.

The feeling of guilt does not always go away instantly, but we
can take God at His Word and say, "I am forgiven, and the guilt
has been removed." Our feelings will eventually catch up with our
decisions. We can live by the truth in God's Word and not the way
we feel.

Power Thought: I receive what Christ did for me. I am
forgiven; the guilt has been removed.

Feed Good Attitudes

And now, dear brothers and sisters, one final thing. Fix your
thoughts on what is true, and honorable, and right, and pure,
and lovely, and admirable. Think about things that are excellent
and worthy of praise.   PHILIPPIANS 4:8 NLT

Our thoughts are the raw materials for our attitudes. It isn't possible for us to treat people in a loving, kind, godly way if we think
unloving, unkind, ungodly thoughts about them. Good attitudes
are fed and kept alive by good thoughts. Bad attitudes are fed and
kept alive by bad thoughts.

We can have good attitudes or we can have bad attitudes; it's
our choice. We can't just wait for a good attitude to show up; we
have to decide what kind of attitude we are going to have. Choose
to have a godly attitude in all circumstances. Say out loud, "My
attitude is my choice."

_____

Power Thought: My attitude is my choice; I choose to
think on praiseworthy things.

You Can Bless Yourself

*So [it shall be] that he who invokes a blessing on himself in the
land shall do so by saying, May the God of truth and fidelity
[the Amen] bless me.*　　　　　　　　ISAIAH 65:16

There is a life principle in the above Scripture you can carry into
every area you desire victory: nobody's words have as much
authority in your life as your own. Learn to bless yourself by speaking only words that contain God's power and will for your life.

Words are containers for power. Proverbs 18:21 says, "Death
and life are in the power of the tongue, and they who indulge in it
shall eat the fruit of it [for death or life]." And with power comes
responsibility. God has given you words, and He expects you to be
accountable for the power carried in them.

Take notice of the things you say throughout your day because
what you say does matter to you and your well-being. When you
speak about your situation, say what you believe Jesus would say,
and you will open the door for the miracle-working power of God.

Power Thought: I am blessed with miracle-working
power.

A Happy Heart Is Good Medicine

A happy heart is good medicine and a cheerful mind works
healing, but a broken spirit dries up the bones.

PROVERBS 17:22

The more I ponder it, the more amazed I am that I can immediately increase or decrease my joy and the joy of others by simply choosing to say good things.

Joy is vital! Nehemiah 8:10 tells us joy is our strength. No wonder the devil works overtime trying to do anything he can to diminish our joy. Don't sit by and let it happen to you. Fight the good fight with faith-filled words, releasing joy into the very atmosphere you are in.

Jesus came to bring good news and glad tidings of great joy, to overcome evil with good. He wants you to be as committed as He is to finding and magnifying the good in everything. Do yourself a favor and say something good!

———————

Power Thought: I can immediately increase my joy by speaking right words.

Don't Miss the Miracle

And she had a sister named Mary, who seated herself at the Lord's feet and was listening to His teaching.

LUKE 10:39

You will not enjoy the present moment and the gifts it contains if you don't have a balanced attitude toward work. Luke 10:38–42 tells the story of Jesus' visit to the home of two sisters, Mary and Martha. Martha was overly occupied and too busy (see Luke 10:40). But Mary sat down at Jesus' feet and listened to what He had to say.

Jesus said Mary made the better choice. Jesus did not tell Martha not to work, but He did tell her not to be frustrated or have a bad attitude *while* she worked. Jesus wants you to work hard, but He also wants you to be wise enough to realize when you should stop all activity and not miss the miracle of the moment.

Power Thought: I have balance in my life. I enjoy my work, and I know when to stop and enjoy other things.

Passing the Test

Beloved, do not be amazed and bewildered at the fiery ordeal
which is taking place to test your quality, as though something
strange (unusual and alien to you and your position) were
befalling you.   1 PETER 4:12

God sometimes allows us to be in less than desirable situations
to test our "quality." Quite often, He is planning a promotion for
us in life if we pass the test in front of us. We are like children in
school who must pass tests in order to be promoted to the next
grade. Are you passing the test—refusing to murmur, complain,
or blame when things don't go your way?

You should praise and bless God while you are in the low val-
leys of life as well as when you are on the mountaintops. If you are
in a difficult or trying situation right now, discipline yourself not
to complain, but instead give praise and glory to God.

Power Thought: I will not complain when trials come my
way.

Thoughts, Words, and Habits

Then He touched their eyes, saying, According to your faith and trust and reliance [on the power invested in Me] be it done to you. MATTHEW 9:29

How do our thoughts and the words we speak affect our habits? In my opinion, they are the starting point for breaking all bad habits and forming all good habits. In fact, thinking and speaking negatively is a bad habit in itself—and one we need to break by beginning to think and speak positively.

You can literally think and talk yourself into victory or defeat. You not only get all the things you think and say, but you can have anything God says you can have in His Word. Jesus told people they would have what they believed, even sight for the blind men (see Matthew 9:27–30). They simply had to believe—to renew their minds to think as God thinks (see Romans 12:2 and Colossians 3:10)—and they could have the blessings God wanted them to have... and so can you!

Power Thought: I believe in God's power that gives me victory over my bad habits.

The God-Shaped Hole Inside You

As for me, I will continue beholding Your face in righteousness
(rightness, justice, and right standing with You); I shall be fully
satisfied, when I awake [to find myself] beholding Your form
[and having sweet communion with You].

PSALM 17:15

There is a God-shaped hole inside every one of us, and even if we
had all the money in the world, there is nothing to be bought that
could fill it. The only thing that is going to fill that craving is God
Himself. Seek God as your first and most vital necessity in life. Put
Him first in your time, thoughts, conversation, and actions. Love Him
with all of your heart and talk to Him throughout the day about
everything that takes place in your life.

As you include Him in all that you do, you will develop an intimacy with Him that will satisfy your soul like nothing else in the
world can do.

———————————

Power Thought: God is the only One Who can satisfy my
craving; I am fully satisfied as I enjoy intimacy with Him.

Be Equipped to Meet Needs

*And God will generously provide all you need. Then you will
always have everything you need and plenty left over to share
with others.* 2 CORINTHIANS 9:8 NLT

God blesses us so we can bless others. He does not want us to
be needy; He wants us to be equipped to help people who are in
need, and we cannot do that if all we are experiencing is lack.
When we don't have enough to meet our own needs and the needs
of our families or others for whom we are responsible, then it is
very difficult to help other people. This is one reason God promises to provide for us and to do so abundantly.

I encourage you to develop the mind-set of a generous giver.
Look for ways to give and for needy people to whom you can give.
Study what the Bible says about God's provision, and see yourself
as one who meets needs.

Power Thought: I am a generous giver.

Healthy Roots Develop Healthy Fruit

May Christ through your faith [actually] dwell (settle down, abide, make His permanent home) in your hearts! May you be rooted deep in love and founded securely on love.

EPHESIANS 3:17

When you become a student of God's Word, you begin to desire a change in your behavior. But so often, as soon as you deal with one bad behavior, another immediately pops up to replace it. Why? Because bad fruit comes from a bad root. For example, as long as we feel bad about ourselves, we will produce bad fruit of some kind. It might be anger, insecurity, fear, or indecision. But it will show up in our behavior. We must deal with the root of the problem. No matter how good things look outwardly, if they are not right on the inside, sooner or later it will be revealed on the outside.

Your worth and value are not based on outward things; they are based on God's love for you. Receive His love, learn to love and value yourself, and you will begin to produce better fruit in your life.

Power Thought: I am rooted and grounded in Christ.

Agree with God

*Acquaint now yourself with Him [agree with God and show
yourself to be conformed to His will] and be at peace; by that
[you shall prosper and great] good shall come to you.*

JOB 22:21

We all want God's promises to come to pass and be a reality in
our lives. Yet many of us say the opposite of what God says in His
Word. Too often we talk about how we feel or what we think when
we should be talking about what God's Word says.

Jesus is the High Priest of our confession (see Hebrews 4:14).
Our confession is merely what we say, and Jesus works accordingly based on our words. He works for us to bring God's will to
pass, but He can work only so far as we agree with God in what He
says. The power of agreement is amazing. Even when we agree as
people, it increases our power significantly, so just imagine what
happens when you agree with God.

Power Thought: I agree with God and want His will for
my life.

Seek First

*But seek (aim at and strive after) first of all His kingdom and
His righteousness (His way of doing and being right), and then
all these things taken together will be given you besides.*

MATTHEW 6:33

When you receive Jesus as your Savior, the first thing He wants
to give you is righteousness. He takes your sin and gives you His
righteousness. God hates for His children to be tormented with
ungodly feelings, questioning whether something is wrong with us
because we don't like what others like or because we can't do what
they do; He gave us His righteousness so we don't have to believe
those thoughts.

You can stop listening to Satan's lies and say instead: "I am in
right standing with God." You can stop thinking, *What is wrong
with me?*, and start letting God show you the good things that He
has placed in you. Believe and speak, "I have right standing, not
wrong standing. I have rightness through Christ when I stand
before God."

Power Thought: I am the righteousness of God in Christ.

God's Way Every Day

[I assure you] by the pride which I have in you in [your fellowship and union with] Christ Jesus our Lord, that I die daily [I face death every day and die to self].

1 CORINTHIANS 15:31

What did Paul mean when he said, "I die daily"? Paul faced the possibility of physical death every day, but Paul was also saying he had to say no to himself and his fleshly desires every single day. *Every day* he had to stop doing things his way in order for God's will to be done.

Twenty years after his conversion, Paul wrote, "It is no longer I who live, but Christ (the Messiah) lives in me" (Galatians 2:20). It took Paul *twenty years* to get to the place where he was no longer living for himself, so don't feel bad if you haven't yet arrived. Say, "I'm not where I need to be, but thank God I'm not where I used to be. I'm okay, and I'm on my way!"

Power Thought: I will say no to selfishness *every day* so I can live God's way.

Start Your Day Right

*Listen to my voice in the morning, LORD. Each morning I bring
my requests to you and wait expectantly.*

PSALM 5:3 NLT

Many times the way your day starts is the way it is going to go all
day. This is why the devil tries so hard to get us in a bad frame of
mind early in the day. Have you found the enemy trying to make
you mad, using something—anything—to get your mind full of
sour thoughts before the day has really started? He tries to get you
upset about traffic or the *possibility* of a long line at the bank or the
doctor's office before you have even left your house!

But you can make your mind up early in the morning to enjoy
each aspect of your day, whether everything goes the way you
planned or not. The mind is the battlefield. Start choosing right
thoughts early in the morning, and you will begin to walk in victory.

———————————

Power Thought: I wake up *expecting* to enjoy my day.

Created in God's Image

And put on the new nature (the regenerate self) created in
God's image, [Godlike] in true righteousness and holiness.

EPHESIANS 4:24

The devil is a faultfinder. If you focus on only what is wrong in life, with yourself and other people, then you are taking your nature from him. However, God has given you a new nature. If you are truly His child, you can learn to function from the renewed part of your being.

The Bible says we are to put off the old man and put on the new man, who is re-created in Jesus Christ (see Ephesians 4:22–24). As you follow the leading of your renewed spirit and the Holy Spirit who dwells in you, you will develop new habits, but it does take time. God operates on the principle of "gradual growth"—things changing little by little. Rather than focusing on how far you still have to go, recognize instead how far you have come. Staying positive will help you in all areas of life.

———————

Power Thought: I have a new nature; God is changing me to reflect His image.

Realistic Expectations

Each time he said, "My grace is all you need. My power works best in weakness." So now I am glad to boast about my weaknesses, so that the power of Christ can work through me.

2 CORINTHIANS 12:9 NLT

How we treat ourselves is often how we treat others. For example, if you receive God's mercy, then you will be able to give mercy to others, but if you are demanding and never satisfied with yourself, you will be the same way with others.

We need to learn to be good to ourselves and yet not be self-centered. You should respect and value yourself; you should know what you are good at and what you are not good at and realize God's strength is perfected in your weaknesses. We stress over our faults and yet everyone has them. If you had no faults, you would not need Jesus, and that is never going to happen!

Power Thought: I have realistic expectations of myself and others.

Emotions Are Here to Stay

Be self-controlled and alert... standing firm in the faith.
1 PETER 5:8–9 NIV

We all have emotions, and we always will; they are part of being human. Since that is true, I believe emotional stability should be one of the main goals of every believer. We should seek God to learn how to manage our emotions and stop them from managing us.

I urge you to make emotional maturity a priority in your life. If you do not believe you are doing a good job of managing your emotions, begin to pray and seek God for emotional maturity. I also encourage you to learn what upsets you the most or prompts you to behave emotionally and be watchful during those situations.

Power Thought: I have control over my emotions.

Our Words Are Seeds

Nothing in all creation is hidden from God. Everything is naked and exposed before his eyes, and he is the one to whom we are accountable.   HEBREWS 4:13 NLT

Every action is a seed we sow, and we will reap a harvest from our seeds. Our words, thoughts, attitudes, and actions are all seeds that we sow, and seeds produce harvest. Sow mercy; reap mercy. Sow judgment; reap judgment. Sow kindness; reap kindness. If you don't like how your life is right now, I have good news for you. You can change your life by sowing right seeds.

If you're not in a good place in life, you didn't make one wrong choice to end up where you are, and you can't make one right choice to get yourself out of it. Change won't happen overnight. But if you invest your life in learning what is the right thing to do and then do it with God's help, you will reap the harvest.

Power Thought: With God's help, I'm sowing good seeds every day of my life.

The Work of the Holy Spirit

*Therefore, [there is] now no condemnation (no adjudging guilty
of wrong) for those who are in Christ Jesus.*

ROMANS 8:1

The Holy Spirit is given to us for many reasons, and one of the
really important ones is to convict us of sin—not to condemn or
make us feel guilty, but to teach us how to be lifted out of sin. We
should love and appreciate all conviction because without it, we
could easily live lives of self-deception. Spiritually mature persons
can receive conviction and not let it condemn them. Correction
from God is never rejection. The fact that He is unwilling to leave
us as we are is a sign of His love for us, and He works daily to
change us into His image and help us develop His character.

Power Thought: God does not condemn me or condone
my sins, but He does convict me so I may be changed into
His image.

God Doesn't Play Favorites

[In this new creation all distinctions vanish.]

COLOSSIANS 3:11

God does not show favoritism (see Acts 10:34). He desires to bless *all* people and see all of their needs met abundantly. If people see themselves as always living in poverty, they are not giving God an opportunity to work in their lives. God loves all people equally and wants the best for all of us, not just some of us.

God has not assigned His children to an upper class, a middle class, and a lower class. The world may think like that, but God does not, and you shouldn't either. The promises of God are for "whosoever will" (see John 3:16–17). *Whoever* will believe in God and serve Him wholeheartedly can be blessed *in any way*, just as much as anyone else can be blessed. With God, there are no distinctions, and He shows no partiality (see Galatians 2:6 and Acts 10:34–35).

Power Thought: God sent His Son for ME!

A Place of Peace

In peace I will both lie down and sleep, for You, Lord, alone make me dwell in safety and confident trust.

PSALM 4:8

Worry is like sitting in a rocking chair, rocking back and forth; it's always in motion and it keeps us busy, but it never gets us anywhere. In fact, if we do it too long, it wears us out!

Trusting God allows us to enter His rest—a place of peace where we are able to enjoy life while we are waiting for Him to solve our problems. He cares for us; He will solve our problems and meet our needs, but we have to stop thinking and worrying about them.

I realize this is easier said than done, but there is no time like the present to begin learning a new way to live without worry, anxiety, and fear.

—————————

Power Thought: I am free from worry and reasoning; I rest in the Lord.

Take Control of Your Anger

He who is slow to anger is better than the mighty, he who rules his [own] spirit than he who takes a city.

PROVERBS 16:32

This verse illustrates the power of controlling your anger. God gave us self-control (see Galatians 5:23) to monitor our mouths, thoughts, passions, emotions, and tempers, yet many people don't know that controlling their emotions is an option. They think the way they feel must dictate their actions. When they get mad, they let the feeling of anger decide how long they will stay angry, and all the while it is stealing their joy from them. In Scripture, we read about Absalom, who held on to his anger for *two years*, allowing it to build until he ended up killing his own brother (see 2 Samuel 13).

You need to know that with God's help, you can get over your anger. Study the Word about anger and the importance of forgiving those who hurt you, and pray and ask God to give you grace and strength to forgive (see 2 Corinthians 12:9). Don't let anger shut down the power of God in your life.

———————

Power Thought: I forgive quickly and never allow emotion to rule my actions.

The Foundation for Security

*For God made Christ, who never sinned, to be the offering
for our sin, so that we could be made right with God through
Christ.*   2 CORINTHIANS 5:21 NLT

A sense of security is something everyone needs and desires.
Security enables us to enjoy healthy thinking and living. It means
we feel safe, accepted, and approved of. When we are secure, we
approve of ourselves, we have confidence, and we accept and love
ourselves in a balanced way.

I believe it is God's will for each one of us to be secure. The foun-
dations for security are knowing who we are in Christ, accepting
God's unconditional love, and accepting ourselves even though we
realize we have weaknesses and are not perfect. Remember, when
God looks at you, He sees the righteousness of His Son, Jesus.

Power Thought: I know who I am in Christ and what I
believe.

The Mind of Christ

Let this same attitude and purpose and [humble] mind be in you which was in Christ Jesus: [Let Him be your example in humility:].   PHILIPPIANS 2:5

We often have problems in our relationships because our minds are full of pride. We may think more highly of ourselves than we do other people when the Bible tells us we should do the opposite— we should always think more highly of other people than we do ourselves. That doesn't mean you should have a bad attitude about yourself, but it does mean you shouldn't think you're better than somebody else.

Pride was Satan's sin: all he said was "I, I, I, I." But the Bible says we are to have the mind of Christ. Jesus had a humble mind. He thought about Himself in a balanced way. The Bible says even though He was the Son of God, He did not think Himself too good to serve others. God exalts the humble, but the proud He brings down (see 1 Peter 5:5). Take authority over prideful thoughts, and let God help you maintain a humble attitude.

Power Thought: I have the mind of Christ.

Don't Get Stuck in a Moment

*He makes me lie down in [fresh, tender] green pastures; He
leads me beside the still and restful waters. He refreshes and
restores my life (my self).*   PSALM 23:2–3

Your future has no room for your past, and I encourage you not to
get stuck in a moment in your life that is over. God is a Redeemer
and a Restorer. He promises to restore our souls, and He will—if
we invite Him in and cooperate with His healing process in our
lives.

When Psalm 23 says He makes us lie down and leads us beside
still and restful waters, it reminds me that God wants us to have
peace. In order to do that, we need to stop running from the past
and simply make a decision to be still, face the past, and receive
healing from God. As long as we are running, something is chas-
ing us, but if we confront it with God by our side, then we can
defeat it and enjoy the new life that is ours in Christ.

Power Thought: I am looking forward to the bright future
that God has planned for me.

Self-Control

*And in [exercising] knowledge [develop] self-control, and in
[exercising] self-control [develop] steadfastness (patience,
endurance), and in [exercising] steadfastness [develop]
godliness (piety).*   2 PETER 1:6

As believers in Jesus Christ, God has given us a new nature, but at
the same time, we also have to deal with the old nature. When we
allow the old nature to rule, we will follow our feelings instead of
operating in self-control. Self-control is a fruit of our new nature,
and all we need to do is develop it. We can develop self-control by
using it, just as we can develop muscles by using them.

Exercising self-control is a form of freedom. You don't have
to do what you feel like doing. You're free to do what you know
is wise. Discipline and self-control will help you be the person
you want to be. Don't ever say, "I just don't have any self-control,"
because the truth is that you do have it, but it needs to be exer-
cised in order to be strong.

Power Thought: I exercise self-control.

The One Thing You Can Do

*I do not consider, brethren, that I have captured and made it
my own [yet]; but one thing I do [it is my one aspiration]:
forgetting what lies behind and straining forward to what lies
ahead...*   PHILIPPIANS 3:13, emphasis added

Paul knew the one thing that would help him more than anything
was to forget the past.

How do we forget what lies behind us—the situations in our
pasts, especially those things causing us to feel guilty? We stop
thinking and talking about them, and keep pressing forward. We
all have a past, but we also all have a future! Stop living in the past
mentally and emotionally, and believe by faith that good things
are ahead.

Don't focus on things you can no longer do anything about,
and don't waste time in regret. Even though we make mistakes in
life, we can recover and still enjoy an amazing life through Christ.
Get excited! Good things are coming!

Power Thought: My past is the past; God has a good plan
for what lies ahead.

Privilege

*Lean on, trust in, and be confident in the Lord with all
your heart and mind and do not rely on your own insight or
understanding.*   PROVERBS 3:5

Part of trusting God is having unanswered questions. When you
get answers, you don't need to trust God anymore. But if you don't
have answers, then you will need to trust God. He could give us
all the answers to everything, but He doesn't because He wants us
to trust Him.

Have you ever said, "There's nothing we can do but trust God"?
Like it's your last-ditch effort—you've done everything else and
now you're left with no other choice.

We need to change the way we talk. We need to realize trusting
God is the greatest privilege we have. What an honor to be able to
say, "No matter what kind of problem I have in my life, *I get to trust
God*!" God wants to take care of you, but He doesn't start until you
stop. Retire from self-care, and start trusting God.

Power Thought: I don't have all the answers, but God
does. I put my trust in Him.

Excuses, Excuses

But they all alike began to make excuses.   LUKE 14:18

Moses made excuses when God called him to service. He said he wasn't eloquent enough and could not speak (see Exodus 4:10). Felix made excuses when Paul was speaking to him about righteousness and self-control. He essentially said, "Right now is an inconvenient time. Can you come back later?" (see Acts 24:25).

When God invites people into relationship with Him, many people come up with excuses when the truth is they simply don't want to make the sacrifices required to follow Him. Even among those who are believers in Jesus, we still hear ample excuses for not serving Him fully. It is time to deal with excuses and start speaking truth. There is one truth none of us will be able to avoid: The day will come when every person will stand before God and give an account of his or her life (see Romans 14:12). On that day there will be no excuses!

Power Thought: I am accountable for every word I speak.

Perfect Love Casts Out Fear

*There is no fear in love [dread does not exist], but full-grown
(complete, perfect) love turns fear out of doors and expels
every trace of terror! For fear brings with it the thought of
punishment, and [so] he who is afraid has not reached the
full maturity of love [is not yet grown into love's complete
perfection].*   1 JOHN 4:18

Learning about and receiving the unconditional love of God is
what sets us free from fear. Nothing else will! "Perfect love casts
out fear" (1 John 4:18 NASB). Only God has perfect love, and it can
be yours by faith.

Faith expresses itself in love (see Galatians 5:6). How can we
put our trust in God if we are not convinced He loves us at all
times? Take God at His Word and begin to receive His love for you,
which will set you free from all fear.

———————

Power Thought: God's love for me is perfect and
unconditional; I have no fear.

Energize Your Life

And [so that you can know and understand] what is the immeasurable and unlimited and surpassing greatness of His power in and for us who believe, as demonstrated in the working of His mighty strength... EPHESIANS 1:19

Do you ever hear people say, "I'm so tired," or "I wish I had more energy"? This is not God's best for us. God wants us to feel good and have the passion and energy we need to enjoy our lives.

Some people do suffer with conditions requiring medication or therapy due to things they could not avoid. But many times our symptoms are simply a result of not taking good care of ourselves. You are valuable, and I urge you to invest time, energy, and finances in doing things that will keep you healthy. Whether you need to change your eating habits, sleep more, exercise more, reduce stress, or worry less—no matter what it takes—find out why you do not feel well and do something about it. Even if you feel good, you can avoid future problems by taking good care of yourself now!

Power Thought: God's power is in me, energizing me to do His good pleasure!

A Transformed Life

Don't copy the behavior and customs of this world, but let God
transform you into a new person by changing the way you
think. Then you will learn to know God's will for you, which is
good and pleasing and perfect.   ROMANS 12:2 NLT

How are we transformed? According to this Scripture, we are
transformed by learning to think in a completely different way.
This is a large part of being a successful Christian. You will not be
a victorious Christian just because you go to church, own different
translations of the Bible, or have a large library of teaching CDs
and DVDs. You will not have victory unless you learn to transform
your thoughts.

The word *transformed* means "to change into another complete
form, to totally change the appearance of, to convert." I love that
because when people accept Christ as their Savior, we say they
have been "converted." First God converts us, and then He converts everything else in our lives by helping us convert (renew) our
thinking.

_____

Power Thought: God can transform my life by
transforming my thoughts.

The Happiest People on Earth

I came that they may have and enjoy life, and have it in abundance (to the full, till it overflows).

I think some people have a perception of Christianity as a stern, severe, and joyless lifestyle. That's because many who call themselves Christians have sour attitudes and sad faces. They can be critical of others and quick to judge. Those of us who love and serve God and His Son, Jesus Christ, should be the happiest people on Earth. We should be able to enjoy everything we do, simply because we know God is present. God sent Jesus to ensure we would enjoy life. Our joy makes God happy!

Happiness is an emotion that fosters well-being, and it is contagious. One of the best ways to witness to others about Jesus is to be happy and enjoy all you do. Since everyone simply wants to be happy, if they see truly happy Christians, they will be open to learning about and receiving Jesus themselves.

Power Thought: I enjoy every moment of my life.

Pursue Peace

Let him search for peace (harmony; undisturbedness from
fears, agitating passions, and moral conflicts) and seek it
eagerly. [Do not merely desire peaceful relations with God, with
your fellowmen, and with yourself, but pursue, go after them!]

1 PETER 3:11

The Word of God instructs us to desire peaceful relations with God, with ourselves, and with one another. It actually says we are not merely to desire them, but to pursue and go after them.

I like to say the Bible is a book about relationships. It has a great deal to say about our relationship with God—everything starts with the development of our relationship with the Father through His Son, Jesus Christ. God's Word also talks extensively about our relationships with other people—teachings on love, proper attitudes, serving others, and giving abound. The Bible also teaches us about the importance of having a proper attitude toward ourselves.

Receive God's love, and develop a good relationship with yourself. Value yourself and realize that you are created in God's image and that He delights in you. When you have a good relationship of love and acceptance with the Father and with yourself, it will be easy to have good relationships with other people.

———————

Power Thought: I pursue peace in all of my relationships.

Stop Saying "Hate" and Start Saying "Joy"

Let there be no filthiness (obscenity, indecency) nor foolish and sinful (silly and corrupt) talk, nor coarse jesting, which are not fitting or becoming; but instead voice your thankfulness [to God].
EPHESIANS 5:4

Quite often people use the phrase "I hate." They hate driving to work, cleaning their houses, going to the grocery store, cutting the grass, paying their bills, and on and on. I think each time we say we "hate" something, it makes it harder for us to do it with joy the next time.

Start saying by faith that you enjoy those things that are naturally more difficult for you to enjoy. Start saying it in obedience to God, and soon you will find those things to be more enjoyable. We can talk ourselves into things and out of things. You can talk yourself into despising something you need to do, or you can have a good attitude and speak good words about it and make it a lot more pleasant.

Power Thought: I speak life-giving, positive, and thankful words.

Learn and Do

*Pray that the LORD your God will show us what to do and where
to go.... Whether we like it or not, we will obey the LORD our
God to whom we are sending you with our plea. For if we obey
him, everything will turn out well for us.*

JEREMIAH 42:3, 6 NLT

According to the Scripture above, when the Israelites asked
Jeremiah to speak to God on their behalf, they had already decided
they were going to learn what to do, and, no matter what it was,
they were going to do it.

I wonder what would happen if people today had this same
attitude every single time they sat anywhere the Word was being
preached. What would your life be like if every time you went to
church or listened to a teaching CD or read the Bible you had the
mind-set, *Whatever I learn today, I'm going to do it!*

James 4:17 says if we know what to do and don't do it, that is
sin. The wrong things we *commit* are sin, but the right things we
omit are also sin. Make a decision to be a "doer" of God's Word,
and not merely a "hearer."

Power Thought: I obey God promptly.

Authority over the Devil

Behold! I have given you authority and power to trample upon
serpents and scorpions, and [physical and mental strength
and ability] over all the power that the enemy [possesses]; and
nothing shall in any way harm you.   LUKE 10:19

One of the best ways to defend ourselves against the devil is to
know the Word of God and speak it aloud against the lies he bom-
bards our minds with. When the devil tells you God doesn't love
you and you will never amount to anything, go to war using the
Word of God. Get out your two-edged sword and use it!

Talk back to the devil, loud and clear, saying, "I am the righteousness of God in Jesus Christ" (see 2 Corinthians 5:21); "God
has a good plan for my life" (see Jeremiah 29:11); and "Nothing
can separate me from the love of God" (see Romans 8:35–39).
Trust God—know that you are more than a conqueror through
Christ as you confidently declare the truth of His Word.

Power Thought: Through Christ I have authority over
the devil.

Take Inventory

But Jesus said, "You feed them."
"With what?" they asked. "We'd have to work for months to earn enough money to buy food for all these people!"
"How much bread do you have?" he asked. "Go and find out."   MARK 6:37–38 NLT

In Mark 6, the disciples tell Jesus it is getting late and they should send the people away to get themselves something to eat. But Jesus instructs His disciples to feed the people.

The disciples respond, stating they cannot feed five thousand men. Because they felt they couldn't meet the *entire* need, they were choosing to do nothing. But Jesus tells them to go and see what they do have to give.

Instead of focusing on what you can't do or what you don't have or what you've lost, take an inventory of what you *do* have. When you give God the little bit you have, He will do the multiplying and you will end up with more left over than what you started with. Then you'll get to use what you have to help others.

Power Thought: I always have something to offer.

Motivated by Love

The work of each [one] will become [plainly, openly] known
(shown for what it is); for the day [of Christ] will disclose and
declare it, because it will be revealed with fire, and the fire will
test and critically appraise the character and worth of the work
each person has done.   1 CORINTHIANS 3:13

Your reason or motive for doing the things you do is very important. God wants you to have a pure heart. He wants you to do
things because He is leading you to do them or because they
are the right things to do. God wants you to be motivated by love.
You should do what you do for the love of God and humanity.
You should regularly take some time and ask yourself why you are
doing the things you do. It is not *what* you do that impresses God;
He is concerned with the *why* behind what you do. Ask God to
reveal your motives to you and to change any that are not pure.

Power Thought: God sees in me a pure heart; my motives
are not hidden from Him.

Eliminate *Worry* from Your Vocabulary

Therefore I tell you, do not worry about your life.... Who of you by worrying can add a single hour to his life?
MATTHEW 6:25, 27 NIV

I wonder how many times the statement "I'm worried about..." is spoken each day. Millions of people use this phrase, but what is the point of it? Does worry change anything? No. So why keep doing it?

Start listening to yourself and other people, and each time you hear "I'm worried," say to yourself, *Worry is useless, and I refuse to do it.* If we thoroughly realize the foolishness of it, maybe we will stop saying it and doing it.

Instead of saying, "I'm worried," replace those negative, useless words with "I trust God." When you say you trust God, His power is released to work in your life. Study God's Word, remember His faithfulness to you in past situations, and be determined to stop wasting your time worrying.

Power Thought: I trust God; I do not waste my time with worry.

Be Decisive

I am speaking as to intelligent (sensible) men. Think over and make up your minds [for yourselves] about what I say. [I appeal to your reason and your discernment in these matters.]

1 CORINTHIANS 10:15

Some people make decisions too quickly, others make them too slowly, some make them unwisely, and some don't make them at all. Life is filled with decisions; we all make numerous decisions daily. We decide how late we will sleep, what we will eat, what we will wear, and what we will do with our time. We make employment decisions, relationship decisions, financial decisions, and, most importantly, we make spiritual decisions. Even people who won't make decisions are still making a decision not to decide.

If we make right spiritual decisions—deciding to put God first in all things—then the rest of our decisions will be easier. Making decisions in a wise and timely manner is vital to our peace and success in life.

Power Thought: I have discernment to make wise decisions.

Worry or Worship?

And you shall be to Me a kingdom of priests, a holy nation [consecrated, set apart to the worship of God].

EXODUS 19:6

Worry and worship are polar opposites, and we would be much happier if we learned to become worshippers instead of worriers. Worry creates an opportunity for the enemy to torment us, but worship (reverence and adoration of God) leads us into His presence, where we will always find peace, joy, and hope. God created us to worship Him, and I don't believe we can overcome the pressures and temptations in our lives if we don't become worshippers.

Don't waste another day of your life worrying. Determine what your responsibility is and what it is not. Don't try to take on anything that is God's responsibility. When we have a problem, we should do what we can do and then trust God to do what we cannot do. So give yourself and your worries to God, worship Him, and begin enjoying the abundant life He has for you.

Power Thought: I wasn't created to worry; I was created to worship.

You Are Righteous

*For if because of one man's trespass (lapse, offense) death
reigned through that one, much more surely will those who
receive [God's] overflowing grace (unmerited favor) and the
free gift of righteousness [putting them into right standing with
Himself] reign as kings in life through the one Man Jesus Christ
(the Messiah, the Anointed One).*   ROMANS 5:17

God wants us to think, speak, and behave rightly, so He gives us
what we need in order to do those things. God will never require
us to do something without giving us what we need to do it. God
gives us the gift of righteousness so we can become righteous in
what we think, say, and do!

Although we have sinned, our sins cannot be compared to the
righteousness of God's free gift. Our sin is great, but His free gift
of righteousness is greater.

The fruit of your life cannot be any greater than what you
believe you are, so you must learn to think about and believe in
your righteousness in Christ. If you think all the time that something is wrong with you, then you will keep producing wrong
things, but believing you're right with God will help you produce
right behavior.

Power Thought: I am in right standing with God.

God's Word Is Filled with Power

*So shall My word be that goes forth out of My mouth: it shall
not return to Me void [without producing any effect, useless],
but it shall accomplish that which I please and purpose, and it
shall prosper in the thing for which I sent it.*

ISAIAH 55:11

Isaiah teaches us that the Word coming out of God's mouth
(which I believe can also be our mouths when we speak His Word)
will not return without accomplishing what it was sent to do. The
Word of God is seed, and when we release it in the earth, we will
see good results (see Isaiah 55:10–11).

We are God's representatives on the Earth, His mouthpieces,
and we are instructed by the apostle Paul to imitate Him (see
Ephesians 5:1). As His representative, you should speak His Word
just the same as He would. Speak it boldly, with authority, believing it has power to change your life and circumstances.

Power Thought: When I speak the Word, it has the power
to accomplish God's desired purposes.

Desiring to Please Him in All Things

For the eyes of the Lord run to and fro throughout the whole earth to show Himself strong in behalf of those whose hearts are blameless toward Him.   2 CHRONICLES 16:9

Anyone who loves God wants to please Him. Just having the desire to please Him pleases Him. A desire to please God is necessary—it motivates us to seek His will in all things. People who have a deep desire to please God may not perform perfectly all the time, but they keep pressing forward and always have the attitude of wanting to improve.

In 2 Chronicles 16:9, we see God is searching to and fro for someone whose heart is perfect toward Him. The Scripture does not say He is looking for someone with a perfect performance, but rather someone with a perfect heart—a heart desiring to please Him.

Power Thought: I desire to please God.

Only a Fool Hates Discipline!

The reverent and worshipful fear of the Lord is the beginning and the principal and choice part of knowledge [its starting point and its essence]; but fools despise skillful and godly Wisdom, instruction, and discipline.

PROVERBS 1:7

Some people cringe at the mention of the word *discipline*. They have a mental attitude toward it that is unhealthy and self-defeating. We need to see that discipline is our friend, not our enemy. It helps us be what we say we want to be, do what we say we want to do, and have what we say we want to have.

Discipline doesn't prevent you from having fun and doing what you want to do in life, but instead it helps you obtain what you *truly* want, which is peace, joy, and right relationships. Learn to love discipline (it will keep you out of trouble!), and embrace it as your companion in life.

Power Thought: I love discipline; discipline helps me receive God's perfect plan for my life.

On-Purpose Thinking

But certain individuals have missed the mark on this very matter [and] have wandered away into vain arguments and discussions and purposeless talk.   1 TIMOTHY 1:6

The Bible teaches us that our words have power and we get exactly what we speak. Along with that, our thoughts affect our moods and attitudes. In other words, your attitude in life affects your altitude in life, meaning your attitude determines how far you can go in life—how far you can go in pursuing your dreams, relationships, business, etc.

Your thoughts and my thoughts will determine the kind of lives we will have in the future. And you don't have to think about and focus on whatever falls into your head. You can think things on purpose. Sometimes it is good to just sit down and have a think session. And then it's good to have a confession session. After almost forty years of knowing these things, I still have to practice them daily. Be determined to maintain good thoughts.

_____

Power Thought: I think and say things on purpose.

Read and Reap

[Things are hidden temporarily only as a means to revelation.]
For there is nothing hidden except to be revealed, nor is
anything [temporarily] kept secret except in order that it may
be made known.   MARK 4:22

The Word has tremendous treasures, powerful life-giving secrets
that God wants to reveal to us. They are manifested to those who
ponder, study, think about, practice mentally, and meditate on the
Word of God.

There is no end to what God can show you out of one verse of
Scripture. You can study a Scripture one time and get one thing,
and another time you'll see something else you did not even notice
before.

The Lord keeps revealing His secrets to those who are diligent
about studying the Word. Don't be the kind of person who always
wants to live off of someone else's revelation. Study the Word
yourself, and allow the Holy Spirit to bless your life with truth.

Power Thought: Revelation is available to me when I
study God's Word.

Get a New Attitude

*I have strength for all things in Christ Who empowers me [I am
ready for anything and equal to anything through Him Who
infuses inner strength into me; I am self-sufficient in Christ's
sufficiency].*   PHILIPPIANS 4:13

There may be times in our lives when God allows us to go through
serious difficulties to enable us to eventually minister to and comfort others who are suffering. If this is what God permits in our
lives, then we can be assured we are able to handle it because He
promises never to allow us to go through more than we can bear.

It may feel as if we're never going to overcome the challenges
we're facing, but if we look back at the lives of believers in past
centuries, we see that God gave them the strength to overcome the
"impossible." Let's remember how David faced Goliath, and take
joy in defeating obstacles rather than letting them defeat us.

———————————

Power Thought: I am able to do whatever I need to do in
life because Christ lives in me.

Never Give Up on Those You Love

Love bears up under anything and everything that comes, is
ever ready to believe the best of every person, its hopes are
fadeless under all circumstances, and it endures everything
[without weakening]. Love never fails [never fades out or
becomes obsolete or comes to an end].

1 CORINTHIANS 13:7–8

Refuse to give up on people. Whether you are believing for someone you love to become a Christian, change behavior, leave a bad
relationship, stop using drugs, go back to school, come home, or
get a job, keep believing change is possible. Do not give up on the
ones you love; your patient love and faithfulness may be exactly
what they need to make a complete turnaround.

God is love (see 1 John 4:8), and He never gives up on us. So
choose to live with the same attitude. Believe in the power of love
to change and transform anything and anyone.

———————

Power Thought: My love for others is unfailing; I will
never give up on the people I love.

God's Best

Every good and perfect gift is from above, coming down from the Father of the heavenly lights, who does not change like shifting shadows.   JAMES 1:17 NIV

The apostle James says we are discontent because we try to get what we want by our own means rather than asking God for it and trusting Him completely. We see what others have and become jealous, which creates discontentment in our hearts. We should want only what God wants us to have and believe that if we ask for something and don't get it, the reason is because He has something better for us in mind.

Even if you don't have what you want or need right now, be content with what you do have, refuse to focus on what you don't have, spend a lot of time being a blessing to others, and stay hopeful concerning what you want and need. Remember, God is faithful and His timing is perfect!

Power Thought: I want God's good and perfect plan for my life.

Leave It in God's Hands

*"What do you mean, 'If I can'?" Jesus asked. "Anything is
possible if a person believes."*   MARK 9:23 NLT

In this verse, Jesus says all things are possible "if a person
believes"—not "if a person comes up with a bright idea and a big
plan and thinks about it over and over, trying to make it work in
his or her own power."

We all have something going on in our lives we would like to
see change for the better—desiring change is just part of living.
But the truth is you can't really change most of your circumstances
or yourself without God's help. Put your desire before God in
prayer and ask Him to work in you and in your life in amazing
ways. Always be ready to do anything He asks you to do, but don't
frustrate yourself by trying to do things without Him.

_____

Power Thought: I believe all things are possible
with God!

Absolute Faith

For we have heard of your faith in Christ Jesus [the leaning of your entire human personality on Him in absolute trust and confidence in His power, wisdom, and goodness] and of the love which you [have and show] for all the saints (God's consecrated ones).   COLOSSIANS 1:4

God's will is for us to live by faith. You might be thinking of how far you have to go in order to be all God wants you to be, and you feel overwhelmed. Your mind wants to think, *This is just too much; I will never be able to do all He needs.*

This is where faith comes in. You can think, *I don't know how I am going to do it, but I am expecting God's help. With God, all things are possible.*

Just get started and keep going day after day. Be encouraged by any progress you make and refuse to be discouraged by how far you think you still have to go. God is pleased that you are on your way to perfection (see Philippians 3:12).

Power Thought: I have absolute faith, trust, and confidence in God.

Medicine for Your Soul

He will not always chide or be contending, neither will He keep His anger forever or hold a grudge.   PSALM 103:9

When someone mistreats me, I initially feel angry, then I spend the next few minutes or hours, depending on the seriousness of the mistreatment, getting the emotion under control by talking to God. When you feel angry, consider these appropriate actions: talk to yourself about how foolish it is to let some unkind person ruin your day, and then follow Scripture and pray for the person who hurt you. Decide to believe the best of the person who offended you, and try to get your mind off the offense and onto something more pleasant. It is also helpful to remember that we also do things that hurt people, and often without even intending to do so. Obeying and meditating on the Word of God is medicine for our souls. It brings not only instruction, but comfort in every situation.

———————

Power Thought: I am slow to anger and quick to forgive.

Don't Give the Devil an Opening in Your Life

I will not talk with you much more, for the prince (evil genius, ruler) of the world is coming. And he has no claim on Me. [He has nothing in common with Me; there is nothing in Me that belongs to him, and he has no power over Me.]

JOHN 14:30

This verse teaches the importance of not speaking rashly out of our emotions. Jesus told His disciples He would be leaving the world very soon. The suffering He was about to endure was unimaginable, but Jesus was determined not to speak words that would give Satan an opportunity to hinder the plan of God.

Nothing takes more self-control than not speaking negatively in a negative situation. The mouth wants to spurt out everything it thinks and feels. But in times like that, you need to go deeper, thinking and speaking out of your renewed spirit. These are important times to agree with God and say what He says in His Word.

———

Power Thought: I will not talk in ways that give the devil power.

Be the One God Is Searching For

*And you, Solomon my son, know the God of your father
[have personal knowledge of Him, be acquainted with, and
understand Him; appreciate, heed, and cherish Him] and
serve Him with a blameless heart and a willing mind. For the
Lord searches all hearts and minds and understands all the
wanderings of the thoughts. If you seek Him [inquiring for and
of Him and requiring Him as your first and vital necessity]
you will find Him; but if you forsake Him, He will cast you off
forever!*   1 CHRONICLES 28:9

God is looking for people who are passionate about the things He
is passionate about. He is looking for people who will wholeheartedly pursue Him. He is also looking for people who will love others at their jobs, in their neighborhoods and homes, and help the
lost, the poor, and the needy. In short, God is looking for people
He can work with and through. If you are willing to put aside self-
will and start wanting what God wants, then you are the type of
person He is searching for.

Power Thought: I wholeheartedly desire to be used by
God.

The Righteousness of God

But no weapon that is formed against you shall prosper, and every tongue that shall rise against you in judgment you shall show to be in the wrong. This [peace, righteousness, security, triumph over opposition] is the heritage of the servants of the Lord [those in whom the ideal Servant of the Lord is reproduced]; this is the righteousness or the vindication which they obtain from Me [this is that which I impart to them as their justification], says the Lord.

ISAIAH 54:17

God sees us as valuable and worthy—we know this because He sent His Son, Jesus, to die for us. Part of our inheritance as believers is to be secure—to know who we are in Christ, to have a feeling of righteousness or rightness with God. The devil likes to remind us of what we are not, but God delights in affirming us and reminding us of who we are and what we can do through Jesus. Even when you're being attacked by adverse circumstances, remember that God is for you and that you are right with Him.

Power Thought: I am valuable because of who I am in Christ.

Patience Grows under Trial

In the world you have tribulation and trials and distress and
frustration; but be of good cheer [take courage; be confident,
certain, undaunted]! For I have overcome the world. [I have
deprived it of power to harm you and have conquered it for
you.]   JOHN 16:33

Patience is a fruit of the Spirit we desperately need in our lives. But
when we pray for patience, we often experience challenges that
give us opportunity to develop patience. We may not like it, but
God has something good in mind—He is actually answering our
prayers and we just don't realize it.

God wants us to bless Him at all times, not just when things
are going our way. When challenges arrive in your life, remember you can be peaceful, enjoy the journey, have faith, and learn
patience because Jesus is with you at every moment. And He will
bring you through to the other side.

———————————

Power Thought: I keep an attitude of good cheer in all
circumstances because God is with me.

God's Delight

May those who delight in my vindication shout for joy and
gladness; may they always say, "The LORD be exalted, who
delights in the well-being of his servant."

PSALM 35:27 NIV

When you are waiting for your needs to be met, don't fall into the trap of thinking you are being punished for something you have done wrong in your life. God is merciful, He is good, and He *wants* your needs to be met. He *wants* you to have a good job, a decent place to live, transportation to get you where you need to go, good friends, and a great spiritual life. God *wants* you to be blessed in every area of your life—spiritually, mentally, emotionally, physically, financially, and socially.

There are times when we have to wait for the things we want and need, and we should trust God during these times and remain emotionally stable while we are waiting. We all have to wait for things that we want in life. Trust God to be your Vindicator because only He can make wrong things right, and He does so at the right time. While you wait, keep believing and thinking: *God abundantly supplies all my needs; I will get out of debt; the Lord takes pleasure in my prosperity; God gives me favor; He opens right doors for me and closes wrong ones; God wants to bless me, and I'm willing to take it.*

Power Thought: God takes pleasure in my well-being—spirit, soul, and body.

Exceedingly, Abundantly, Above and Beyond

Now all glory to God, who is able, through his mighty power at work within us, to accomplish infinitely more than we might ask or think.   EPHESIANS 3:20 NLT

God never does barely enough; He always does more than enough. He is abundant in loving-kindness, mercy, and forgiveness. Jesus came so we might have life and have it more abundantly (see John 10:10). He is truly a God of abundance.

He is able to do exceedingly, abundantly, above and beyond all we ever dare to hope, ask, or think. In His wisdom, God may not give us everything we want when we want it, but He will always take care of us. Don't minimize Him, making Him small and expecting much less than He desires to give, but see Him as He is; speak of His abundance and expect to be amazed.

Power Thought: God always exceeds my expectations.

Be an Encourager

Treat others the same way you want them to treat you.
LUKE 6:31 NASB

The Bible teaches us to do unto others as we want them to do unto us. Think about what you want and start to give it away. For example, if you want to be encouraged, then be encouraging!

Be careful of your thoughts about people. If you think uncomplimentary or discouraging thoughts, they will usually slip out of your mouth. Instead, look for and magnify the good in every person, and you'll treat people accordingly.

We all love to be encouraged and made to feel really good about ourselves.

Compliments actually help us perform better, while nagging makes us behave worse. Choose a person you would like to have a better relationship with and begin to aggressively encourage and compliment him or her. I believe you will be amazed at how much better he or she responds to you.

Power Thought: I am a very encouraging person.

Creatures of Habit

Do not let yourself be overcome by evil, but overcome (master) evil with good.   ROMANS 12:21

Habits are things we learn to do through repetition so often that we eventually do them unconsciously or with very little effort. When someone is known to do the same thing all the time, we call that person a "creature of habit." Don't be deceived, however, by thinking you can't help what you do, because the truth is you can do or not do anything if you really want to.

One of the ingredients of forming good habits and breaking bad ones is focusing on what you *want* to do and not on what you want to *stop* doing. For example, if you overeat and want to form balanced, healthy eating habits, don't read cookbooks that are filled with beautiful, mouth-watering desserts, but instead read a good book on nutrition that will educate you on how to make better choices.

Don't defeat yourself before you even begin by setting your mind on the wrong things. Set your thoughts on what you want, and you will achieve your goal.

Power Thought: I will overcome bad habits by concentrating on and forming good ones.

Open Your Mouth

*David said to the Philistine, "You come against me with sword
and spear and javelin, but I come against you in the name of
the LORD Almighty, the God of the armies of Israel, whom you
have defied. This day the LORD will hand you over to me, and
I'll strike you down . . . and the whole world will know that there
is a God in Israel."*   1 SAMUEL 17:45–46 NIV

Like David, we all have enemies or what we call *giants* in our lives
who need to be defeated. First Samuel 17:42–48 tells us that when
David was preparing to do battle with the giant Goliath, he ran
toward him (not away from him), with the power of God as his
weaponry, confessing *out loud* what he believed the end result of
the battle would be.

We can easily see from David's example how we should approach
the enemies we face in our own lives: we must open our mouths
and speak the Word of God. You don't ever have to be afraid of the
giants in your life because the greatest One lives in you, and you can
release His power by boldly speaking out your faith in Him.

***

Power Thought: I use the weapon of God's Word to
defeat my enemies.

A Case of the "Ifs"

Set your minds on things above, not on earthly things.

COLOSSIANS 3:2 NIV

Do you have a bad case of the "ifs"? It is a common misconception that *if only* we had this, that, or the other, we would find the happiness and fulfillment we so desperately desire. We find ourselves saying things like: *If* I didn't have to work, *if* we had more money, *if* I had a bigger house, *if* the kids were grown, *if* I were married, *if* I weren't married . . .

Stop thinking that you could be happy "if" your circumstances were different, and start being happy right now because God loves you and has already blessed you in many ways. Our unhappiness usually comes from within us and not from something around us. So I recommend that you take responsibility for your own joy and stop blaming the lack of it on anything or anyone. The people who are happy are the ones who decide to be happy.

Power Thought: God has blessed me, and I am happy!

Tell God Everything

Evening and morning and at noon will I utter my complaint
and moan and sigh, and He will hear my voice.... But I will
trust in, lean on, and confidently rely on You.

PSALM 55:17, 23

David was not hesitant when it came to telling God exactly how he felt. But he also followed up by saying he trusted God to be faithful to keep His promises. Often David would even remind God of something He had promised in His Word.

I believe it was spiritually and even physically healthy for David to express to God how he really felt. It was a way of releasing his negative feelings so they could not harm his inner man while he was waiting for God's deliverance. Sometimes we need an outlet for the pain we feel in life, and it might help to simply take time to tell God all about it. He already knows, but telling Him can be a good release for you. After telling Him all about how you feel, always follow up by telling Him you trust Him to make all things right and ask for His help to live by His Word, not your feelings.

Power Thought: I can tell God how I feel, and He will never reject me.

Get Rid of the Mixture

The prophet who has a dream, let him tell his dream; but he
who has My word, let him speak My word faithfully.

JEREMIAH 23:28

God is faithful. We can always expect Him to do what He says
He will do. He doesn't do it part of the time, but all the time and
every time. There is never a moment when God doesn't keep His
promises.

We should also be faithful all the time to do what we know to
do. Don't speak positively when you are with your friends from
church but at home revert to words of fear, worry, and doubt. Get
rid of the mixture of positive and negative, words of faith and fear,
and be committed to speaking the right thing all the time. Saying
the right thing occasionally won't give you victory. But when you
are relentless and you speak the Word faithfully, then you will be
in agreement with God and see amazing results in due time.

Power Thought: My words are full of faith every time I
speak.

Joy in All Circumstances

All the days of the desponding and afflicted are made evil [by anxious thoughts and forebodings], but he who has a glad heart has a continual feast [regardless of circumstances].

PROVERBS 15:15

Our joy doesn't come from our circumstances. No matter what comes up in your life, you can have a positive attitude. Set your mind ahead of time so no matter what comes up, you will look for the good in it, find some joy in the midst of it, and enjoy your life.

God is positive, so you should be too. Face every day with excitement, believing something good will happen. And if it doesn't, believe it for the next day. Make an announcement out loud to the devil: "I will outlast you!" There's good in everything if you'll just look for it. The minute you decide to have a more positive attitude, you will begin to feel more joy in your life.

Power Thought: I have a positive, upbeat, excited, and passionate attitude in all circumstances.

The Lord Is My Rock

The Lord is my Rock, my Fortress, and my Deliverer; my God, my keen and firm Strength in Whom I will trust and take refuge, my Shield, and the Horn of my salvation, my High Tower.   PSALM 18:2

Why do you think Jesus is referred to as "the Rock"? Because He is stable and never-changing, just like a rock. Jesus Christ is the same yesterday, today, and forever—and we're supposed to imitate Him.

Waiting to see how you feel each day is never a good idea. Has anyone ever invited you to do something and you responded, "Let me wait and see how I feel"? That just gives the devil room to make sure you *don't* feel like doing what you need to do or what can benefit you. We will sometimes have unpleasant times, but we don't have to live by our feelings; we can choose to stand firm and be stable when we find our strength in the One Who never changes.

Power Thought: In Christ, I am strong and stable.

The Holy Spirit Is an Encourager

And I will ask the Father, and He will give you another
Comforter (Counselor, Helper, Intercessor, Advocate,
Strengthener, and Standby), that He may remain with you
forever.   JOHN 14:16

God obviously knows how important encouragement is because
He sent us a Divine Comforter and Encourager when He sent the
Holy Spirit. The Holy Spirit is the *Parakletos*, the Greek word for
"One Who walks alongside us, giving aid, encouraging, building
us up, edifying, and comforting us."

God comforts us in our time of need so we might then comfort
others in theirs. God always expects us to give away what He gives
us. This is a spiritual law, and it is the way to keep a steady flow of
whatever we need coming into our lives. The more we encourage
others, the more encouraged we will be ourselves (see Luke 6:38).
Make a decision that you will encourage everyone you are with
today. When we live to be blessings, we will be blessed in return.

Power Thought: The Holy Spirit is always available to
comfort and encourage me.

Help Hurting People

He who despises his neighbor sins [against God, his fellowman, and himself], but happy (blessed and fortunate) is he who is kind and merciful to the poor.   PROVERBS 14:21

Helping the poor and those who are less fortunate than we are is not only a nice thing to do, but according to the Bible, it is our responsibility. God cares deeply for the poor and needy and seems to have a special place in His heart for the widow and the orphan because they are alone and unable to meet all their needs. God gives us hearts of compassion, but when needs arise we can't close our hearts—we need to open our hearts and our hands wide to help the poor.

When we give to the poor, the Bible says that we lend to the Lord. Anything we give to help hurting people, God will always return many times over. Not only will He meet our needs, but our joy will increase as a result of giving in love. I urge you to share what you have with those who are less fortunate than you are.

Power Thought: I am always merciful and generous to the poor.

Peace beyond Understanding

And God's peace [shall be yours, that tranquil state of a soul assured of its salvation through Christ, and so fearing nothing from God and being content with its earthly lot of whatever sort that is, that peace] which transcends all understanding shall garrison and mount guard over your hearts and minds in Christ Jesus.   PHILIPPIANS 4:7

Don't be the kind of Christian who is up emotionally when you are getting your way and down when you're not; up when you receive the blessing you've been praying for and down when God hasn't brought it into your life yet.

Accept God's peace, which is beyond understanding, and be content regardless of your "earthly lot." Learn to think, *Even if I don't get my way, I will be happy; I will not let my circumstances control my moods.* When you don't get your way, you can be just as happy as if you did; you have God's peace.

Power Thought: God has given me His peace.

Sing a New Song

*O sing to the Lord a new song, for He has done marvelous
things; His right hand and His holy arm have wrought salvation
for Him.*   PSALM 98:1

Your thought life is directly related to your attitude. In other
words, what you think secretly in your heart is expressed in your
words, facial expressions, and attitude. Would you rather be around
people who have rotten attitudes or people with humble attitudes,
thankful attitudes, positive attitudes, and responsible attitudes?

Take an attitude inventory. If your attitude was a song, would
it be "Make the World Go Away," "Raindrops Keep Falling on My
Head," "I Did It My Way," or "Oh, What a Beautiful Morning"?

Fresh, new ways of thinking will produce a fresh, new attitude,
and that will enable you to sing the Lord a new song.

Power Thought: I will sing to the Lord a new song, for He
is doing marvelous things in my life!

God Wants You to Be Encouraged

He Who began a good work in you will continue until the day of Jesus Christ [right up to the time of His return], developing [that good work] and perfecting and bringing it to full completion in you.

PHILIPPIANS 1:6

God wants us to be *en*couraged, not *dis*couraged. When discouragement and condemnation try to overtake you, examine your thought life. What kind of thoughts are you thinking?

Remember, you become what you think. Think discouraging thoughts, and you'll get discouraged. Change your thinking, and be set free! Instead of thinking negatively, think like this: *I believe God. I believe He is working in me no matter what I may feel or how the situation may look. The Lord has begun a good work in me, and He will bring it to full completion.*

I recommend that you not only purposely think right thoughts, but that you go the extra mile and speak them aloud as your confession.

Power Thought: The Lord has begun a good work in me, and He will bring it to full completion.

God Sees the Good in You

[He exclaimed] O my love, how beautiful you are! There is no flaw in you!   SONG OF SOLOMON 4:7

God loves you and sees the good in you. He sees what you are becoming and what you will be. He is not overly concerned about your faults; He knew all of them when He invited you to be in an intimate relationship with Him. All He wants is your love and a willingness to grow in Him.

Your presence is a present to the world. You are unique and one of a kind. Do not ever forget, for even a day, how very special you are!

Power Thought: God loves me unconditionally, even when I make mistakes.

A Tree with No Fruit

And he noticed a fig tree beside the road. He went over to see if there were any figs, but there were only leaves. Then he said to it, "May you never bear fruit again!" And immediately the fig tree withered up.   MATTHEW 21:19 NLT

When the fig tree has leaves, it also has fruit under the leaves. Jesus saw the leaves on the fig tree and went to it for something to eat because He was hungry. When He saw that it had leaves but no fruit, He cursed it, and I believe He cursed it because it was a phony.

Our words and actions should bear good fruit (see Matthew 7:15–20). If we appear to have good fruit, it is important that we actually have it because people will be watching us to see if we are genuine. God has chosen us to be His ambassadors (see 2 Corinthians 5:20), and we represent Him well when there is good fruit in our lives. It isn't enough just to have a Jesus sticker on our cars and a cross hanging around our necks displaying our Christianity—we must have the fruit to back it up.

Power Thought: I represent God with my words and actions; my life bears good fruit.

Get a Goal

He is the rewarder of those who earnestly and diligently seek Him [out].   HEBREWS 11:6

Think of an area in your life in which you need to refuse to give up. Come up with a goal—one that will require you to be disciplined and overcome some obstacles, but one that also promises great reward. It may be as basic as making your bed each morning, or as ambitious as running a marathon or climbing Mount Everest. It may be to break free from a fear of flying or a fear of public speaking, or it may be to overcome an addiction of some kind. It may be cleaning your house or getting out of debt. Just make sure you and God are in agreement, depend on Him for the strength to do it, and then go after your goal with everything in you.

Be full of holy determination—not some kind of fleshly determination or willpower—but true God-given determination. You do have self-control. It is a fruit of the Spirit, and it is in you—believe it and begin walking in it.

Power Thought: I pursue my goals with diligence and determination.

Go to God First

In all your ways know, recognize, and acknowledge Him, and
He will direct and make straight and plain your paths.

PROVERBS 3:6

I encourage you to form a habit of going to God in prayer the moment anything troubles you.

Brother Lawrence, a monk who lived in the seventeenth century, enjoyed a close, intimate relationship with God; he knew God's Word and His ways, and he always consulted God when he was troubled. He desired to follow God in all things.

The more we grow in God's Word and the more experience we have with His ways, the less we will need to go to other people for advice. It is not wrong to get counsel from the right person or people, but you can also develop a close relationship with God that will help you to spiritually discern your course of action in most situations.

Power Thought: I go to God first, and He directs my steps.

The Rest We Have in God

Come to Me, all you who labor and are heavy-laden and
overburdened, and I will cause you to rest. [I will ease and
relieve and refresh your souls.]   MATTHEW 11:28

It's easy to have peace when there's nothing to be upset about.
Even unbelievers have peace during easy times. But rest found in
God is the gift that keeps believers peaceful during times of trou-
ble. It is a gift from Him to His children.

Jesus said, "Peace I leave with you; My [own] peace I now give
and bequeath to you. Not as the world gives do I give to you" (John
14:27). His peace is a spiritual peace, and His rest is one that operates in the midst of a storm—not in the absence of a storm. Jesus
did not come to remove all opposition from our lives, but rather to
empower us to go through times of opposition peacefully.

Power Thought: I can rest in God and keep my peace no
matter what is going on in my life.

Think Differently

Repent (think differently; change your mind, regretting your sins and changing your conduct), for the kingdom of heaven is at hand.   MATTHEW 3:2

The Amplified Bible describes repentance as changing your mind for the better. True repentance is not saying, "I'm sorry I got *caught* in sin"; true repentance means "I'm going to *change* my mind. I'm going to *turn away* from that kind of behavior, and I'm going to *seek* a new life in Christ." *Repentance* means "to turn and go in another direction." It means to turn away from sin and turn toward God.

After you repent, don't waste your time in guilt and condemnation. God understands our nature and He is patient with us, but we also have to be patient with ourselves. It is immature to beat yourself up every time you make a mistake. Spiritually mature people know they aren't going to be perfect, and they know what to do when they do make mistakes—repent, commit to thinking differently, receive God's forgiveness, and go on.

Power Thought: I repent of my sins, and my mind is renewed by the Word of God to think right.

Our Work Is to Believe

For in the Gospel a righteousness which God ascribes is
revealed, both springing from faith and leading to faith
[disclosed through the way of faith that arouses to more faith].
As it is written, The man who through faith is just and upright
shall live and shall live by faith.   ROMANS 1:17

Our work—the work God asks of each believer—is simply to believe. We are accepted because of our *faith*, not our good works. Christians are referred to as "believers." If our job was to achieve, we would be called "achievers." We often want to place an emphasis on what we do, but our focus should be on what God has done for us in Jesus Christ.

God loves us and accepts us unconditionally. His love is not based on our performance. The Bible says in Ephesians 1:6 (KJV) that we are made acceptable in the Beloved. It was through the sacrifice of the Beloved (Jesus) that we were *made* acceptable, not that we *achieved* acceptance. God loves us no matter what, but it is our *faith* in Jesus that makes us acceptable to God and pleases Him, not our performance.

Power Thought: I live by faith in Jesus Christ.

Acceptable Words

Let the words of my mouth and the meditation of my heart be
acceptable in Your sight, O Lord, my [firm, impenetrable] Rock
and my Redeemer.   PSALM 19:14

It is acceptable to God when we use our mouths to bring joy, love, and good to others. It is not acceptable to God when we use our mouths to bring hurt and destruction. We are still acceptable to Him, but our behavior isn't because it will not produce the good results in our lives that God desires for us.

Ephesians 4:29 teaches us not to use our words to cause the Holy Spirit any grief and gives clear instructions concerning what grieves Him: "Let no foul or polluting language, nor evil word nor unwholesome or worthless talk [ever] come out of your mouth, but only such [speech] as is good and beneficial to the spiritual progress of others, as is fitting to the need and the occasion, that it may be a blessing and give grace (God's favor) to those who hear it."

Properly chosen words can actually change lives for the better. What you say can tear down or build up, so choose words that are agreeable with God's will.

Power Thought: My words are wholesome and acceptable to God.

Hope in the Lord

The Lord said to Abram after Lot had left him, Lift up now your
eyes and look from the place where you are, northward and
southward and eastward and westward.

GENESIS 13:14

In Genesis 13, we see that Abram (whom God later renamed Abraham) had a good attitude—a generous and giving attitude—
toward his nephew, Lot. Abram had a right to the land, but he told
Lot to choose his portion, and Lot chose the best land for himself.
God then told Abram to look from the place where he was. God
didn't say to look *at* where he was; He said to look *from* it—beyond
it—to all God had in store for him. God had a plan for Abram,
even though he had just experienced great loss.

Anytime you need encouragement, you can turn to Jeremiah
29:11 and get it: " 'For I know the plans I have for you,' declares
the LORD, 'plans to prosper you and not to harm you, plans to give
you hope and a future' " (NIV). God wants you to have hope. He's
got a good plan for your life.

Power Thought: I can see from where I am that my future
is bright!

Let Your Yes Be Yes

Let your Yes be simply Yes, and your No be simply No; anything more than that comes from the evil one.

MATTHEW 5:37

There was a time not too far in the past when a person's word was his honor; to not keep one's word was unthinkable. When people made a business deal, a twenty-page contract covering every minute thing imaginable was not necessary. They simply came to an agreement and shook hands.

Having integrity requires you to be honest and do the right thing in every situation. You cannot make others do what is right, but you are responsible to God and yourself to do right. You must never be the kind of person who says, "Everyone else does it (lies, cheats, etc.), so what's the problem?" Even if nobody in the whole world kept their word, you should still keep yours, simply because it is the right thing to do.

Power Thought: I am true to my word.

Overcoming Indecision

[He has given us a spirit] of power and of love and of calm and
well-balanced mind and discipline and self-control.

2 TIMOTHY 1:7

Many people struggle with indecision (the inability to make a decision) and double-mindedness (constantly changing their minds)
because of fear or a lack of confidence. However, you can make a
decision and stick with it because you have discipline and a calm,
well-balanced mind.

You can easily feel overwhelmed by all the decisions you need
to make daily unless you have confidence in your ability to make
right ones. Don't ever say again, "I have a hard time making decisions," because when you think and speak like that you are setting
yourself up for confusion. Instead, you can believe the next time
you need to make a decision that you will hear from God, be led
by the Holy Spirit, and know what to do. Even if you have had difficulty doing so in the past, this is a new day for you, and you are
in charge of your thinking—it is no longer in charge of you!

Power Thought: My mind is calm, and I'm in control of
my thinking.

It's Not So Hard

I press on toward the goal to win the [supreme and heavenly]
prize to which God in Christ Jesus is calling us upward.

PHILIPPIANS 3:14

Be careful how you talk about any habit you are trying to break.
Don't go out with friends and talk about how you are trying to
break such-and-such bad habit and it is *so hard*. The more you say
it is hard, the harder it will be. Actually, you would be better off
not to talk about it much at all. Keep your goal between you and
God, and possibly one or two other trusted friends or family mem-
bers whom you want to pray for you and encourage you.

When you are weary of doing battle with your wrong desires,
think of how wonderful it will be when the bad habit is a thing of
the past and a new habit has taken its place. Focusing on developing the good habit you want to establish will automatically help
you enjoy freedom from the bad habit.

Power Thought: I will press on until I reach my goal and
enjoy the reward when I've received the prize!

Idle Words

But I tell you, on the day of judgment men will have to give account for every idle (inoperative, nonworking) word they speak.   MATTHEW 12:36

An idle word is a word that is useless. It's a word that does nothing. If it does anything at all, it usually hurts somebody. To a large degree, the lives we have now are the results of thoughts we've meditated on in the past and words we've spoken. It's not due to bad luck or the devil being after us. Much of it is related to the way we think and the way we speak.

If you realize you're thinking about something that is not fruitful, the best way to interrupt a thought pattern is to speak what you want to think about. For example, if I find myself thinking, *People don't treat me right, and I am not happy about it*, I can interrupt that thought pattern by thinking, *The people in my life are not perfect, but I am not either, and I am blessed in many ways*. Choose wise thoughts and words!

Power Thought: I choose to speak positive, faith-filled words that agree with God.

Don't Look Back

Escape for your life! Do not look behind you or stop anywhere in the whole valley; escape to the mountains [of Moab], lest you be consumed. GENESIS 19:17

Lot and his family lived in a city consumed by wickedness. God was angry at the degradation in the city and decided to destroy it. He sent two angels to Lot's house to tell him to take his family and flee and not look back. Lot's wife made the mistake of disobeying the command, and she looked back. Right then and there, she turned into a pillar of salt.

Jesus doesn't want us to forget what happened to this woman, so in Luke 17:32, He spoke these three words: "Remember Lot's wife!" In other words, "Stop looking back. The past is finished. Look to the future ahead!" Begin to see, think on, and talk about the future God has planned for you (see Jeremiah 29:11), and you will soon make progress in the right direction. If there is anything you need to let go of, there is no better time than now!

Power Thought: I am looking forward and making progress toward the good future God has planned for my life.

Take Responsibility

The man replied, "It was the woman you gave me who gave me the fruit, and I ate it."

Then the LORD God asked the woman, "What have you done?"

"The serpent deceived me," she replied. "That's why I ate it."

GENESIS 3:12–13 NLT

Excuses have been used by humans to avoid responsibility since time began. After Adam and Eve sinned in the Garden of Eden, Adam blamed Eve (and God for giving him Eve), then Eve blamed the devil. People make excuses for their sin all the time instead of simply admitting it, confessing it, and asking God to forgive them for it.

Excuses can easily become lies, causing us to break the commandment that tells us not to lie (see Exodus 20:16). When we make excuses, we are lying to ourselves, God, and others. You can easily find a reason for every error, but it is better to take responsibility for your actions. Remember: "The Truth will set you free" (John 8:32).

Power Thought: I do not make excuses; I am honest in my speech and take responsibility for my actions.

Feed My Lambs

When they had finished eating, Jesus said to Simon Peter,
"Simon son of John, do you truly love me more than these?"
"Yes, Lord," he said, "you know that I love you."
Jesus said, "Feed my lambs."   JOHN 21:15 NIV

What are you doing to help someone else? Are you making a difference in someone's life? Because that is how you show your love
for God. The cycle of love God pours into your life is not complete
until it is pouring out of you to meet other people's needs.

If love has no action to back it up, then it becomes empty words
with no power. God proved His love for us by giving His only Son
to die for our sins. And we can prove our love for God by letting
Him use us to help other people (His sheep). Don't wait to feel like
being a blessing; rather, start doing it on purpose, and you will
realize that it adds joy to your life.

Power Thought: I love God, and I enjoy sharing His love
with other people.

Be "God Loves Me" Minded

God is love, and he who dwells and continues in love dwells and continues in God, and God dwells and continues in him.

1 JOHN 4:16

I remember when I began my ministry. When I was preparing for my first meeting, I asked the Lord what He wanted me to teach, and what came to my heart was, *Tell My people I love them.*

"They know that," I said. "I want to teach them something really powerful, not a Sunday school lesson out of John 3:16."

The Lord reminded me that if people really knew how much He loved them, they would act differently than they do.

As I began to study the subject of receiving God's love, I realized I was in desperate need of the message myself. I had a subconscious, vague sort of understanding that God loved me, but I needed deeper revelation. The love of God is meant to be a powerful force in our lives, one that will take us through even the most difficult trials without our ever doubting God's love.

Power Thought: I am actively aware of God's love for me.

Angry Words

But now put away and rid yourselves [completely] of all these things: anger, rage, bad feeling toward others, curses and slander, and foulmouthed abuse and shameful utterances from your lips!   COLOSSIANS 3:8

Anger is one of our strongest emotions; it grows and manifests in words and actions. We all experience anger, and feeling anger is not a sin—it is what we do with the anger that is important.

When you experience the emotion of anger, you shouldn't act on those feelings. Don't be led and motivated by them. Don't say what you would like to say or do what you would like to do, because that is what gets you into trouble. Instead, follow the guidance of the Holy Spirit and the Word of God, and do what you believe Jesus would do in the same situation you are facing.

You may be thinking, *But I can't help it; I'm angry!* The truth is that you feel anger, but you don't have to let it control your behavior.

It's important to understand something about emotions: What goes up always comes down. Emotions are fickle, and what bothers you today might affect you quite differently tomorrow. Wait for emotions to subside and then decide what you should say and do.

Power Thought: I will not speak carelessly out of my anger.

God Wants to Bless You

The Lord is my Shepherd [to feed, guide, and shield me], I shall not lack.   PSALM 23:1

Being able to maintain a good attitude during times of suffering is a virtue, and it is very important, but continual suffering is not God's will for anybody. The apostle Paul said he had times of being abased and times of abounding (see Philippians 4:12). We will go through difficulties in this life, but we can, and should, expect God's deliverance along with a return to the abundant life.

We must never see God as a stingy god who would withhold something we need. Certainly, there are times when we don't get what we want when we want it, but if that happens, God has a good reason. Perhaps the timing isn't right, or we are not mature enough to handle it yet, or He has something better in mind, but it is never because He doesn't want us to be blessed. That thought simply isn't consistent with who He is.

———————————

Power Thought: The Lord is my Shepherd; I have all I need.

Life Isn't Fair, but God Is Faithful

*He is the Rock, His work is perfect, for all His ways are law and
justice. A God of faithfulness without breach or deviation, just
and right is He.*   DEUTERONOMY 32:4

Life isn't fair, but God is faithful. He heals the wounds and bruises
of the brokenhearted. We may not know why things happen the
way they do, but we can know God. We can know His love, forgiveness, and mercy. When we are sad and emotionally distraught,
one of the very simple yet profound things that helps is this: to
look at and be thankful for the good things you do have rather
than dwelling on the injustices you've suffered. You might think,
I've heard that a thousand times! But are you doing it? Knowledge
without action is useless. Trust God's love for you and His faithfulness in your life, and choose to be thankful!

Power Thought: God is just and faithful; His ways are
perfect.

The Spirit Inside You

For God is working in you, giving you the desire and the power to do what pleases him.   PHILIPPIANS 2:13 NLT

God's Spirit is working in you. You can relax and let His Spirit do a *thorough* work in you, changing your thoughts and attitudes until you can see all things and people the way God sees them. Even when you are doing your worst, God believes the best in regard to you, and He works with you to bring the best out of you.

Start by thinking, *God loves me unconditionally. He has given me His Spirit and put a new heart and attitude in me. Everything in my spirit is good and positive and full of faith.* Anytime you do anything sinful, you should immediately ask God to forgive you and decide to go in a new direction. You shouldn't ignore the wrong things you do—always ask for forgiveness—but you should see and celebrate what you do right.

Power Thought: God sees the best in me, and He is working to bring it out.

Forgiveness Is Forever

For by a single offering He has forever completely cleansed and perfected those who are consecrated and made holy.... He then goes on to say, And their sins and their lawbreaking I will remember no more.   HEBREWS 10:14, 17

God's forgiveness is *forever*—ongoing for the duration of our lives; it is for every day. When Jesus died on the cross, He not only forgave everything we had done in our pasts, but He also committed Himself to forgive and forget every sin we would commit in the future.

He knows our thoughts before we think them; He knows our words before they come out of our mouths; He knows every wrong decision we will ever make—and they're all covered. All we have to do is stay in a relationship with Him. After all, what He wants from us more than anything else is not perfect performance, perfect behavior, or perfect attitudes, but hearts that really love Him.

Power Thought: When Jesus died on the cross for me, He covered every sin I will ever commit.

Where the Mind Goes, the Man Follows

For you have need of steadfast patience and endurance, so that you may perform and fully accomplish the will of God, and thus receive and carry away [and enjoy to the full] what is promised.

HEBREWS 10:36

Don't get discouraged if forming a new mind-set seems difficult in the beginning. You may have to say you will trust God and not worry thousands of times before you start to feel the effects of saying so. There's nothing wrong with that! Each time you come into agreement with God in your thoughts and words, you are making progress.

No matter how long it takes for you to renew your mind with these power thoughts, just keep at it because the diligent person succeeds. You are training your mind to work for you instead of against you, which takes faith and patience. Don't forget: Where the mind goes, the man follows.

———————————

Power Thought: I am patient and determined.

God's Promises Already Exist in Your Life

*As it is written, I have made you the father of many nations.
[He was appointed our father] in the sight of God in Whom
he believed, Who gives life to the dead and speaks of the
nonexistent things that [He has foretold and promised] as if
they [already] existed.*   ROMANS 4:17

One of the great privileges we have, but frequently fail to make use
of, is speaking of things that are not yet evident as if they already
exist. For example, God's Word encourages us to say we are strong
even if we are weak (see Joel 3:10). If you believe God has strength
available for you, as His Word says, why keep saying you are weak?

We need to say what God says and do what He does if we want
to follow His plans for us and have what He wants us to have. We
should be confessing God's promises as if they already exist in
our lives (because they do in the spiritual realm!). We are called
to walk by faith and not by sight (see 2 Corinthians 5:7). In other
words, we believe what God says in His Word even more than we
believe what we see.

Power Thought: I trust I will see everything come to pass
in my life that God has promised in His Word.

A Humble Mind

For by the grace (unmerited favor of God) given to me I warn everyone among you not to estimate and think of himself more highly than he ought [not to have an exaggerated opinion of his own importance], but to rate his ability with sober judgment, each according to the degree of faith apportioned by God to him.   ROMANS 12:3

It is easy to get mixed up about humility. Some people think humility means to have a low opinion of ourselves. Paul says not to have an *exaggerated* opinion of your own importance, but he doesn't say to have a *low* opinion. Some people, in an effort to be humble, don't know how to receive compliments graciously. We all need encouragement, compliments, and appreciation.

A good way to handle appreciation without getting into pride is to receive it when it is given, then, at the end of the day, take the compliments you receive to Jesus and say to Him, "I know whatever I do that is good or right is the result of Your working in me, so I offer You all the praise I was given today and I thank You for the encouragement."

————————

Power Thought: Every compliment I have ever received is because of Jesus.

The Weapon of the Word

If you abide in My word [hold fast to My teachings and live in accordance with them], you are truly My disciples. And you will know the Truth, and the Truth will set you free.

JOHN 8:31–32

Two spiritual weapons available to you are praise and prayer. Praise and prayer should both be filled with the Word of God.

Jesus used the weapon of the Word in the wilderness to defeat the devil (see Luke 4:1–13). Each time the devil lied to Him, Jesus responded with, "It is written," and quoted the Word. Likewise, you can use the Word to tear down the strongholds in your mind and defeat the devil.

Learn to fill your prayers and praise with the Word of God by abiding (staying, continuing) in God's Word. Pray, speak, sing, and study the Word, and you will experience victory in all areas of your life.

Power Thought: I have the ability to know the Truth, and the Truth will set me free.

Praying in His Name

*I tell you the truth, my Father will give you whatever you ask
in my name. Until now you have not asked for anything in my
name. Ask and you will receive, and your joy will be complete.*
                                        JOHN 16:23–24 NIV

When our youngest son was still in school, sometimes people
stayed with him when Dave and I traveled. In order for them to get
medical treatment for him if it was ever needed, we had to sign a
legal document stating they had the right to use our names on our
son's behalf—literally to make decisions in our place.

This is exactly what Jesus did for His disciples and, ultimately,
for all who would believe in Him—He gave us the right to use His
name when we go to God in prayer. When we pray in His name,
it is the same as if He were praying. This privilege seems almost
too wonderful to believe! But we can believe it because we have
Scripture to back it up.

Power Thought: I have the privilege and power of praying
in Jesus' name.

Think Yourself Happy

[And it is, indeed, a source of immense profit, for] godliness accompanied with contentment (that contentment which is a sense of inward sufficiency) is great and abundant gain.

1 TIMOTHY 6:6

If I am discontent, I get upset easily, but if I choose to be content no matter what is going on, then my emotions remain balanced. Our thoughts have a lot to do with our moods. Some thoughts improve our moods and increase our level of contentment, and others send our moods spiraling downward, making us unhappy and discontent. We can think ourselves happy, and we can think ourselves sad! How we talk to ourselves also affects our emotions, so if we talk to ourselves properly, we can stay content and emotionally stable.

Trusting God at all times is the pathway to contentment. Even if we don't have all that we want, we can trust God that He will provide what is right for us in His perfect timing.

Power Thought: God is all-sufficient. When I seek Him, I find contentment.

Put On Love

Therefore, as God's chosen people, holy and dearly loved, clothe yourselves with compassion, kindness, humility, gentleness and patience. Bear with each other and forgive whatever grievances you may have against one another. Forgive as the Lord forgave you. And over all these virtues put on love, which binds them all together in perfect unity.   COLOSSIANS 3:12–14 NIV

We are created to receive and give love. If we do anything else, it is like wearing clothes that are too small for us—it's uncomfortable and steals our joy!

God tells us in His Word to put on love. I believe the phrase "put on" means to do it on purpose. We are to clothe ourselves as representatives of God, Who is love (1 John 4:8; 2 Corinthians 5:20). We are instructed to put on behavior that is marked by mercy, compassion, kind feelings, gentle ways, and patience, which is tireless and long-suffering. We are challenged to be people who endure whatever comes with good temper and to readily pardon one another. Stop wearing things that don't fit, things that make you uncomfortable, and put on love!

Power Thought: When I love people, I represent God.

Speak Excellent Things

Hear, for I will speak excellent and princely things; and the
opening of my lips shall be for right things.

PROVERBS 8:6

In this Scripture, Solomon made a decision about how he would
talk, and we should do the same thing. Just as we can direct our
thoughts, we can also direct our words with God's help. We
should choose to speak excellent things.

Our words affect us and the people around us. They also affect
what God is able to do for us. You cannot have a negative mouth
and a positive life. In 1 Peter 3:10, the apostle Peter teaches us that
if we want to enjoy life and see good days—even in the midst of
trials—we must keep our tongues free from evil. What kind of life
do you want? Do you want an excellent life? If so, then you must
be excellent in your choice of words. Change your words, and you
will change your life!

Power Thought: I choose to speak of worthy, important,
noble, and excellent things.

God Tests Our Minds

Oh, let the wickedness of the wicked come to an end, but establish the just; for the righteous God tests the hearts and minds.   PSALM 7:9 NKJV

We test-drive a new car we are considering buying or other products we find in the store. When we do, we might ask some of the following questions: Is the item of good quality and character? Will it sustain everyday wear and tear? Are there any hidden flaws, imperfections, or defects? And if you find an imperfection in your product, you might decide not to make the purchase, ask for a discount, or see if it can be fixed before you buy it.

In the same way, God tries our thinking (see Revelation 2:23) to see if there are any defects in our minds so He can make us into a quality "product"—a person of character He can trust. The test comes as we face pressure, and if we stand firm in the truth we say we believe, then we pass the test; if we don't, we get to take the test over again. God will never give up on us.

Power Thought: The Lord will test my mind and heart, and I welcome His correction.

Seek Treasures Above

If then you have been raised with Christ [to a new life, thus sharing His resurrection from the dead], aim at and seek the [rich, eternal treasures] that are above, where Christ is, seated at the right hand of God.   COLOSSIANS 3:1

The Bible never tells us to seek *things*. It tells us to seek (pursue, crave) the kingdom of God (see Matthew 6:33) and "the [rich, eternal treasures] that are above."

Colossians 3:2 says in order to seek the right thing you must "set your minds and keep them set on what is above (the higher things), not on the things that are on the earth." To keep your mind on things above doesn't mean to sit around all the time thinking about the pearly gates and your mansion in heaven. It means to learn to think with the mind of the Spirit. Even if you are born again, you are not going to experience the abundant life you can have in Christ unless you set your mind to pursue higher things.

Don't think about your problems today. Instead, think about the good plan that God has for your life and expect something good to happen.

Power Thought: I purposefully set my mind to pursue higher things.

The Measure You Give

Be careful what you are hearing. The measure [of thought and study] you give [to the truth you hear] will be the measure [of virtue and knowledge] that comes back to you—and more [besides] will be given to you who hear.   MARK 4:24

Reading or hearing the Word is good, but when we also devote our thoughts to it, we begin to understand it more deeply. The Word of God is filled with power, and it has the ability to change us. Just as good, nutritious food must be chewed well and swallowed for us to benefit from it, the Word of God must be digested and become part of us. Choose a Scripture and meditate on it all throughout the day, and it will get rooted in your heart and be more meaningful to you.

Power Thought: The more thought and study I devote to the Word, the more I will get out of it.

Gifts from Heaven

John answered, A man can receive nothing [he can claim nothing, he can take unto himself nothing] except as it has been granted to him from heaven. [A man must be content to receive the gift which is given him from heaven; there is no other source.]

JOHN 3:27

John the Baptist came to tell people to "prepare the way of the Lord" (John 1:23). That was his purpose on Earth, and he knew it. But John's disciples were trying to create jealousy in John over Jesus' ministry. They said, "Here He is baptizing too, and everybody is flocking to Him!" (John 3:26).

John responded to them by basically saying, "If He is doing that, then God has anointed Him to do it, and it's His time to do it. And if my time's up, then my time's up!" God doesn't want you to be jealous of the gifts He has given others. He wants you to be content and enjoy the gifts He has given *you*.

Power Thought: I am content with the gifts that have been given to me from heaven.

Be a True Worshipper

A time will come, however, indeed it is already here, when the true (genuine) worshipers will worship the Father in spirit and in truth (reality); for the Father is seeking just such people as these as His worshipers.   JOHN 4:23

Worship is so much more than singing songs. It is a condition of the heart and a state of mind. Our worship for God is born in our hearts, it fills our thoughts, and it is expressed through our mouths and through our actions. Worship is about a personal relationship, spiritual intimacy, and passionate expressions of devotion from people who love God with all their hearts.

The Bible says God is seeking those who worship Him in spirit and in truth. He wants us to worship Him in all that we do out of our sincerely devoted hearts. He does not want to be worshipped out of fear, obligation, or religion; true worship is never the result of mere obligation, but a result of intimacy with God.

———————————

Power Thought: I worship God in spirit and in truth.

Do What the Crisis Demands

Therefore put on God's complete armor, that you may be able to resist and stand your ground on the evil day [of danger], and, having done all [the crisis demands], to stand [firmly in your place].   EPHESIANS 6:13

When you are in a difficult situation, do what you know to do, but don't feel pressured to take action if you have no direction from God. Ask God to open your mind to new ways of doing and seeing things. If He shows you something, then do it, and if He doesn't, then remain peaceful and trust that He will work for you and do what you cannot do.

Think and speak, "It is not shameful to not know what to do, nor should I feel pressured that I must 'do something.'" Nobody has all the answers, all the time, except God. Stay peaceful and stand firmly in Christ, trusting Him to guide you.

Power Thought: I remain peaceful in all situations and trust God for guidance.

Thankful in the Midst of Suffering

Thank [God] in everything [no matter what the circumstances may be, be thankful and give thanks], for this is the will of God for you [who are] in Christ Jesus [the Revealer and Mediator of that will].   1 THESSALONIANS 5:18

The Bible encourages us to always be thankful. That's easy when God answers prayers and delivers us from problems, but it isn't always easy when things go wrong. So how can we remain thankful in the midst of suffering?

We can remember other times when God has delivered us from problems and trust Him to do the same thing again. We can also rejoice over things that are *not* wrong in our lives. We are all very blessed, and it is easy to be thankful when we remember our blessings.

We can be thankful to God in obedience to Him. We don't have to wait to *feel* thankful in order to give thanks. Do it by faith and you will not only see God's deliverance, but you will be happier while you wait.

_____

Power Thought: I give thanks to God at all times.

Reprogram Your Computer

Keep my commandments and live, and keep my law and
teaching as the apple (the pupil) of your eye. Bind them on your
fingers; write them on the tablet of your heart.

PROVERBS 7:2–3

What we think and speak, especially if it is frequent, is written on the tablets of our hearts. It is embedded in our hard drives, so to speak. Just as a computer can put out only the information that is programmed into it, our hearts can put out only what is written on them: "For out of the fullness (the overflow, the superabundance) of the heart the mouth speaks" (Matthew 12:34). If you don't like the results you are getting from your computer and hard drive, you don't hesitate to get a new program or a new computer, and that is what you should do with your life. Start rewriting what has been programmed into your heart by choosing what you think and speak.

Power Thought: I think and speak God's Word; His laws are written on my heart.

Do It Afraid

Be strong, vigorous, and very courageous. Be not afraid,
neither be dismayed, for the Lord your God is with you
wherever you go.   JOSHUA 1:9

When God gave Joshua the job of leading the Israelites into the
Promised Land, He told Joshua to "be not afraid." He didn't tell
Joshua that he wouldn't *feel* fear, but that he would have to have
courage *in the face of* fear. He was basically saying, "You will be
attacked by many fears and you will be tempted to turn back, but
you have to keep going forward. *Do it afraid*; keep going forward
and you will arrive at your desired destination."

I am not suggesting we do foolish things, but if we are fully
assured that we have direction from God, then we must press forward no matter what we feel like or what people say. I have often
heard it said that "courage is not the absence of fear; it is progress
in its presence."

Power Thought: I am strong and courageous because
God is with me.

Opportunities Are All around You

*Now to Him Who, by (in consequence of) the [action of His]
power that is at work within us, is able to [carry out His
purpose and] do superabundantly, far over and above all that
we [dare] ask or think [infinitely beyond our highest prayers,
desires, thoughts, hopes, or dreams] . . .*

EPHESIANS 3:20

These words describe God, and if we want to be like Him, we
need to always go the extra mile, always do more than we have to,
always give more than enough, and always be generous.

Because human nature is selfish and self-centered, generous
giving does not come naturally to us. We have to build into our
thinking the mind-set that we are generous—think it and speak it!

Opportunities to give are all around you, and finding out how
you can bless another person is as easy as using your ears. If you
simply listen to people, you'll soon know what they need or would
like.

Power Thought: I am a very generous person.

The Log in My Eye

You hypocrite, first get the beam of timber out of your own eye,
and then you will see clearly to take the tiny particle out of your
brother's eye.   MATTHEW 7:5

Loving people unconditionally is the greatest gift we can give
them (and ourselves). I have learned that one of the secrets to my
own personal peace is to let people be who God made them to be,
rather than try to make people be who I would like them to be. I
do my best to enjoy their strengths and be merciful toward their
weaknesses because I have plenty of my own. I don't need to try to
take the speck out of someone else's eye while I have a telephone
pole in my own.

Make a decision not to look at—or for—flaws. We all have them!
But you don't have to focus on them.

Power Thought: God is merciful to me with my
weaknesses, and I am merciful toward the weaknesses
of others.

Supernatural Favor

When a man's ways please the Lord, He makes even his
enemies to be at peace with him.   PROVERBS 16:7

God will give you favor with people if you ask Him to do so and put your trust in Him. He can cause even your enemies to be at peace with you. The Bible says He changes the hearts of men the way He changes the course of flowing water (see Proverbs 21:1). If God can make a river flow in a specific direction, surely He can change someone's heart toward you.

When God favors you, He gives you things you do not deserve in the natural. But as long as you try to make things happen by the works of your flesh, God will stand back and wait for you to wear yourself out trying to do what only He can do. But if you stop struggling and ask God to take the driver's seat, you can have favor with God—and He will give you favor with others.

Power Thought: I have favor with God and people.

Transform Your Mind

Do not be conformed to this world (this age), [fashioned after and adapted to its external, superficial customs], but be transformed (changed) by the [entire] renewal of your mind [by its new ideals and its new attitude], so that you may prove [for yourselves] what is the good and acceptable and perfect will of God, even the thing which is good and acceptable and perfect [in His sight for you].   ROMANS 12:2

Don't think as the world thinks. If you want to experience the good will of God for your life, you have to learn how to think the way God thinks, see yourself as God sees you, and renew your mind through studying His Word.

Renewing the mind is a process that takes time, but you can get started right away—getting excited each day about the progress that you have made. Learn to agree with all that God says to you in His Word and to disagree with all the lies of Satan. God has a good plan for you, and He desires to release it in your life.

———————————

Power Thought: My mind is being renewed daily, and my life is changing.

Minister to Yourself

Words kill, words give life; they're either poison or fruit—you
choose.   PROVERBS 18:21 *THE MESSAGE*

Our thoughts affect our words, and our words affect our lives—
words have power, and they directly affect our emotions. Words
fuel good moods or bad moods; in fact, they fuel our attitudes and
have a huge impact on our lives and our relationships.

In Proverbs 21:23 we are told to guard our mouths and tongues
to keep ourselves from trouble. Proverbs also tells us, "Death and
life are in the power of the tongue" (18:21). The message cannot
be any clearer: If you speak positive and good things, you minister life to yourself. You increase your joy. However, if you speak
negative words, you minister death and misery to yourself—you
increase your sadness and your mood plummets. You have the
choice between life and death, being positive or negative—so
choose wisely!

Power Thought: I choose to speak life-giving words.

The Lord Our Provider

The young lions lack food and suffer hunger, but they who seek (inquire of and require) the Lord [by right of their need and on the authority of His Word], none of them shall lack any beneficial thing.   PSALM 34:10

It is important to develop what I call an "abundant mind-set"— one that believes God will always provide what we need in every situation. This is God's promise throughout Scripture, and part of His nature is to provide for His children. In fact, in the Old Testament, one of the Hebrew names of God is *Jehovah-Jireh*, which means the "Lord Our Provider."

There is nothing we need that He is not able and willing to provide. He loves us and wants to take care of us. When we love Him and do our best to progressively learn and obey His ways, He will make sure our needs are met. In fact, there is no one He would rather share His blessings with than His children.

Power Thought: The Lord delights in providing for me.

Cast Down Imaginations

Casting down imaginations, and every high thing that exalteth itself against the knowledge of God, and bringing into captivity every thought to the obedience of Christ...

2 CORINTHIANS 10:5 KJV

This Scripture means when you become aware of a wrong thought in your mind, you can choose immediately not to think it. How *often* will you need to make the right choice? The answer is every day, all of your life.

If the thought of needing to do this the rest of your life seems overwhelming to you, look at it as a privilege rather than a duty. Thank God that He has given us the ability to think for ourselves and not merely be stuck with whatever comes into our minds from some random or outside source. We can learn to think according to God's Word, and when we do, we experience the kind of lives that Jesus died for us to have.

Power Thought: I cast down wrong thoughts as soon as I recognize them.

Out of the Heart the Mouth Speaks

You offspring of vipers! How can you speak good things when you are evil (wicked)? For out of the fullness (the overflow, the superabundance) of the heart the mouth speaks. The good man from his inner good treasure flings forth good things.

MATTHEW 12:34–35

Have you ever said something and thought, *Where did that come from?* The truth is it came from down inside you somewhere. You had to think it at some time, or it wouldn't have come out. Proverbs 23:7 says, "For as he thinks in his heart, so is he." What's in our hearts or in our minds ultimately comes out of our mouths. We can find out the true condition of our hearts by listening to ourselves. If you don't like what you are saying, ask God to help you think as He thinks. And pray this prayer from Psalm 51:10: "Create in me a clean heart, O God, and renew a right, persevering, and steadfast spirit within me."

Power Thought: I speak good things from a pure heart.

The Holy Spirit Leads to Peace and Joy

*After three days the officers went through the camp,
commanding the people: When you see the ark of the covenant
of the Lord your God being borne by the Levitical priests, set
out from where you are and follow it.*

JOSHUA 3:2–3

The ark referred to in the Scripture above contained the Ten Commandments, which represent the will of God, and a piece of manna—the same manna with which God fed the Israelites in the wilderness. The manna represents God's presence and His miraculous provision.

On your journey through life, in every situation you can follow the ark (figuratively speaking) just as the Israelites followed the ark (literally). To "follow the ark" in our day is to follow the leading of the Holy Spirit, Who lives within all believers. As you follow Him, you can be assured that you will always have His presence and provision in your life. It is tempting to follow our own thoughts, emotions, or desires, but that will leave us unfulfilled and unsuccessful. Following the Holy Spirit is the way to peace and joy.

Power Thought: I can trust the Holy Spirit to lead me to peace and joy.

The Golden Rule

So then, whatever you desire that others would do to and for you, even so do also to and for them, for this is (sums up) the Law and the Prophets.   MATTHEW 7:12

Many of us learned as children to recite "the golden rule": *Do unto others as you would have them do unto you.* In other words, treat people the way you want to be treated. If you want respect, treat people with respect. If you want people to be patient with you, be patient with people. If you want people to forgive you, be quick to forgive. We learned the rule as children, but do we practice it as adults?

As a Spirit-filled believer, you need to take the initiative to treat people the way you want to be treated, not the way they treat you. Don't wait for someone else to do what is right; be the one who does what is right first. Learning how to treat people well will dramatically change your life.

_____

Power Thought: I treat others with love and respect.

Give God Everything

Before I formed you in the womb I knew [and] approved of
you [as My chosen instrument], and before you were born
I separated and set you apart, consecrating you; [and] I
appointed you as a prophet to the nations.

JEREMIAH 1:5

Invite Jesus into every area of your life. Don't feel you must hide your faults from Him; He knows all about them anyway. Besides, His strength is made perfect in our weaknesses (see 2 Corinthians 12:9). God works through weak, imperfect people so no one can take the credit that is due Him alone. Never doubt that God can use you.

The Lord doesn't see only what we are right now; He sees what we can become. He knows the plans He has for us, and they are plans for progress and success, not defeat and failure (see Jeremiah 29:11).

Power Thought: God approves of me; I have been set apart for His purposes.

The Lord Our God Is One

Hear, O Israel: the Lord our God is one Lord [the only Lord].
DEUTERONOMY 6:4

In the Old Testament, the Israelites seemed to make a big deal out of God being "one" (see Psalm 50:1 and Malachi 2:10). Why?

The pagans of their day were deceived into believing there was a god for everything—to have a baby, they talked to the god of fertility; to grow crops, they talked to the god of the harvest. All these different gods required different sacrifices for healing, peace, or whatever the people lacked. Can you imagine how complicated that must have been?

That's why it was such good news when the one true God revealed Himself and told the people that He satisfied all of their needs. So if you need peace, if you need righteousness, if you need hope, if you need joy, if you need healing, if you need finances— whatever you need, simply go to the one true God.

Power Thought: I go to the one true God, and He meets all of my needs.

He Is with You

Don't be afraid, for I am with you. Don't be discouraged, for I am your God. I will strengthen you and help you. I will hold you up with my victorious right hand.   ISAIAH 41:10 NLT

No matter what your fear is, God's Word says you are not to fear because He is with you. It is just that simple. I am sure the question comes to mind: *If God is with me, why do bad things happen?* God never promises us trouble-free lives, but He does promise us His presence and the strength (mental, physical, and emotional) we need to get through our troubles.

Whatever the problem is, you can be assured it will pass, God will be with you all the way through it, and you will be stronger and know God better when it is over than before it began.

Power Thought: God is with me at all times, so there is no need to be afraid.

I Can't Help It!

*I have strength for all things in Christ Who empowers me [I am
ready for anything and equal to anything through Him Who
infuses inner strength into me; I am self-sufficient in Christ's
sufficiency].*

PHILIPPIANS 4:13

As you begin to change the things in your life that are unfruit-
ful and causing you problems, the devil will offer you many
excuses to stay the way you are. One of the things you can expect
to hear in your head is, *I can't help what I think—the thoughts just
come whether I want them or not. I can't help it!* While it is true that
thoughts come without being invited, it is not true that you cannot do anything about them. God's Word teaches us to cast down,
or refute, wrong thoughts (see 2 Corinthians 10:5). That simply
means you shouldn't allow them to stay in your mind. You can get
rid of any thought you don't want by simply deciding to think on
something else.

Power Thought: I have strength in Christ to think godly
thoughts and refute wrong thoughts.

Remain Stable

For you have been granted [the privilege] for Christ's sake not only to believe in (adhere to, rely on, and trust in) Him, but also to suffer in His behalf. PHILIPPIANS 1:29

God needs to be able to depend on us. People need to be able to depend on us. If we ever want to have any self-respect, we need to be able to depend on us too!

When you have a problem, if you are determined to remain stable, the enemy will see it as a clear sign he is defeated (see Philippians 1:28), and it will be a sign to God to bring deliverance in your life. When you have a problem, stand still and see the salvation of the Lord. Remain stable and do the right thing even while the wrong thing is happening to you.

While you are remaining stable and waiting for God's deliverance, you are going to go through some suffering. But the hard things you go through bring victory into your life.

Power Thought: It is a privilege to suffer on Christ's behalf and trust God to bring me to victory.

Free in Christ

*In [this] freedom Christ has made us free [and completely
liberated us]; stand fast then, and do not be hampered and held
ensnared and submit again to a yoke of slavery [which you have
once put off].*   GALATIANS 5:1

As your relationship with God matures, you will find yourself living less by rules and regulations and more by the desires of your
heart. As you learn more of the Word, you will find His desires filling your heart, and it will be easier for you to discern God's will.
God wants you to know His heart well enough that you will want
to follow the prompting, leading, and guidance of the Holy Spirit.

Once you are free in Christ, stand fast in that liberty and do not
become ensnared with legalism, which is the yoke of bondage you
have put off. God wants to bring you into a new place, a place full
of freedom to follow your heart.

Power Thought: I am free to live for Christ.

What Does God Say about Your Past?

*Do not [earnestly] remember the former things; neither
consider the things of old. Behold, I am doing a new thing!*

ISAIAH 43:18–19

Many people are stuck in the past. If they have done something
bad or something bad has happened to them, they believe they
can never get beyond it. This is exactly what the devil wants people to believe, but according to God's Word, it is not true. We *can*
recover from bad things in our pasts, and God will even work good
out of those things. God is a Redeemer, which means He takes
anything bad in us or in our lives and turns that into something
beautiful. No matter what you did in the past or what was done
to you, I challenge you to start saying, "I am forgiven, God has a
good plan for my life, and I will never look back."

Power Thought: I can move on from my past because
God is doing a new thing in my life.

Choose Life

I call heaven and earth to witness this day against you that I have set before you life and death, the blessings and the curses; therefore choose life, that you and your descendants may live.

DEUTERONOMY 30:19

You and I will have many choices to make throughout our lives. In Deuteronomy 30:19, the Lord told His people that He set before them life and death and told them to *choose* life.

Thousands upon thousands of thoughts are presented to you every day. Once you decide to be like-minded with God, then, with the help of the Holy Spirit, you will need to *choose* and *continue to choose* right thoughts that line up with His Word and His will for your life.

Our thoughts become our words, and our words become our actions. Therefore, it is vitally important that we *choose* life-generating thoughts. When we do, we will begin to enjoy the lives Jesus wants us to live.

Power Thought: I choose to think life-generating thoughts.

Do Not Covet

You shall not covet your neighbor's house, your neighbor's wife,
or his manservant, or his maidservant, or his ox, or his donkey,
or anything that is your neighbor's.   EXODUS 20:17

When we judge others for what they own—their houses, cars, jewelry, clothes—it is usually because we are unhappy with what we have (or don't have), not with what they have. For example, if you are speaking badly of a person's car—it is too expensive, or how frivolous the owner must be—then you may really be saying, "I'm not happy with *my* car; I am jealous, and I want your car."

Have you ever heard about a blessing someone received and thought, *When is that going to happen to me?* Instead of being unhappy or jealous or envious when God blesses someone with something you would like to have, be happy for them and let their blessing be an encouragement to you, believing that what God did for them, He can also do for you.

Power Thought: I am happy for others to receive God's blessings. If God can do it for them, He can do it for me too.

Freely and Lightly

I'll show you how to take a real rest. Walk with me and work with me—watch how I do it. Learn the unforced rhythms of grace. I won't lay anything heavy or ill-fitting on you. Keep company with me and you'll learn to live freely and lightly.

MATTHEW 11:29–30 THE MESSAGE

Living "freely and lightly" in the "unforced rhythms of grace" sounds good, doesn't it? I'm sure you have had enough heavy stuff in your life; I have too, and I want to always enjoy being free. It's nice to know you don't have to worry about things, figure out everything, or carry the burdens in your life. It is actually quite refreshing when I realize I don't need to know everything about everything!

We need to get comfortable with saying, "I don't know the answer to this dilemma, and I'm not going to worry about anything because God is in control, and I trust Him. I'm going to rest in Him and live freely and lightly!"

Power Thought: I trust God with the heavy stuff while I live freely and lightly.

Wait for the Lord

But those who wait for the Lord [who expect, look for, and hope in Him] shall change and renew their strength and power; they shall lift their wings and mount up [close to God] as eagles [mount up to the sun]; they shall run and not be weary, they shall walk and not faint or become tired.

ISAIAH 40:31, emphasis added

When success does not come easily, when we find ourselves frustrated and weary in our efforts, we need to wait for the Lord. Waiting for the Lord simply means spending time with Him, being in His presence, meditating on His Word, worshipping Him, and keeping Him at the center of our lives.

When you wait on the Lord, you draw everything you need from Him. He is your refuge, your enabler, your joy, your peace, your righteousness, and your hope. He gives you everything you need to live in victory over any circumstance. Stay close to Him and receive the strength you need every day. Don't let anything separate you from the love of God found in Christ Jesus.

Power Thought: I wait on God daily and look to Him to be my Source of strength in all of my circumstances.

Gather Up the Fragments

When they had all had enough, He said to His disciples, Gather
up now the fragments (the broken pieces that are left over), so
that nothing may be lost and wasted.   JOHN 6:12

Don't just give God what you are and what you feel you have to
offer—give Him what you are not. If you make mistakes or feel
that you are lacking in several areas, give it to God and let Him be
your all. If you give God everything you are and everything you are
not, He will give you everything He is and has. Victory is not about
what you can do; it's about what God can do *through* you.

Paul said that God's strength was made perfect in his weakness. Jesus said to gather up the fragments so nothing is wasted.
If you will give Jesus all of you, even the worn-out, used-up fragments, He will make something awesome out of them. Let God
begin to flow through your strengths and your weaknesses.

Power Thought: Everything I am, and everything I'm not,
can be used by God for His purposes.

Pressing toward Perfection

I don't mean to say that I have already achieved these things or that I have already reached perfection. But I press on to possess that perfection for which Christ Jesus first possessed me.

PHILIPPIANS 3:12 NLT

It is our job to press *toward* the mark of perfection, and yet the Bible teaches us we will not attain perfection until Jesus, the Perfect One, comes to take us to live with Him for eternity (see 1 Corinthians 13:9–10). We can grow; we can change and do better and better. But if we obtained perfection in our behavior, we would no longer need Jesus—and that is never going to happen.

We can, however, have perfect hearts toward God by fully wanting His will and doing all we can to work with the Holy Spirit toward that goal. God sees your heart, and He counts you as perfect even while you are making the journey toward perfection.

Power Thought: I am pressing on toward the goal of perfection in Christ.

No Excuses

*And the Angel of the Lord appeared to him and said to him, The
Lord is with you, you mighty man of [fearless] courage.*

JUDGES 6:12

In the book of Judges, God decided to work through a man named
Gideon to deliver the Israelites from captivity. But when the angel
came to call Gideon, Gideon began rehearsing a list of his inabili-
ties, including reasons why he thought he could not do what God
was calling him to do.

In Judges 6:14 God says, "Have I not sent you?" In other words,
"Would I ask you to do something I haven't equipped you to do?"
And again, in the next verse, Gideon responds with excuses—I'm
too poor, too small, too weak. Because words have power, Gideon
believed what he said about himself more than the encouraging
words of the Lord.

Stop thinking of excuses or things to complain about—*It's too
hard; I've never done this before; this isn't what I had planned; I don't
know how; I'm too old/young; I don't feel like it; I'm afraid*—and start
doing what God is telling you to do.

Power Thought: I can do whatever God asks me to do—
no excuses—because He is with me.

Slow Is Good

Understand [this], my beloved brethren. Let every man be quick to hear [a ready listener], slow to speak, slow to take offense and to get angry. For man's anger does not promote the righteousness God [wishes and requires].

JAMES 1:19–20

In these verses, God is telling us to listen more than we talk. Think about it: If God wanted us to be quick to speak and slow to listen, He would have created us with two mouths and only one ear!

God is also telling us not to easily get offended or angry. If you have a quick, bad temper, start listening more and talking less. Slow is good. Read everything you can get your hands on about managing anger. Repeat over and over in your mind: *I am quick to listen and slow to speak, slow to anger, and quick to forgive.* Trust God to help you manage the feelings of anger. It is vitally necessary for you to be able to control this emotion if you want to enjoy the life God has in mind for you.

Power Thought: I am quick to listen and slow to speak, slow to anger and quick to forgive.

Be Happy Even If You Are Suffering

But even in case you should suffer for the sake of righteousness,
[you are] blessed (happy, to be envied). Do not dread or be
afraid of their threats, nor be disturbed [by their opposition].

1 PETER 3:14

According to this Scripture, you can be happy even if you are suffering, as long as you are suffering for the sake of righteousness. Why? Because God is just, and even though you are being persecuted for doing the right thing, in the end you will win, because when you sow right seeds you will reap a good harvest.

What sense would it make for the Bible to say you are to be envied when you are persecuted unless you had a huge reward coming? Justice means everything wrong is made right. When you suffer for doing the right thing, God will give you double for your trouble (see Isaiah 61:7) because God always blesses those who do the right thing.

Power Thought: God's reward is greater than any suffering I will endure for a season.

Do What Is Right

But he who practices truth [who does what is right] comes out into the Light; so that his works may be plainly shown to be what they are—wrought with God [divinely prompted, done with God's help, in dependence upon Him].

JOHN 3:21

Doing the right thing in all situations should always be our choice, even when we do not feel like doing so. For example, if people have hurt you, then you may not feel like being nice and talking to them, but if you choose to do what is right, then God will heal your emotions. Our part is to pray for the people who hurt us and continue treating them the way we believe that Jesus would treat them.

We usually want to feel better first, but God wants us to do what is right first, no matter how we feel. Doing the right thing while we feel wronged is extremely important for spiritual growth. When we do the right thing when it's hard or we're still hurting, we grow spiritually and will enjoy more emotional stability the next time we are faced with a difficult situation.

Power Thought: With God's help, I can do what is right regardless of how I feel.

God Strengthens You

Fear not [there is nothing to fear], for I am with you; do not look around you in terror and be dismayed, for I am your God. I will strengthen and harden you to difficulties, yes, I will help you; yes, I will hold you up and retain you with My [victorious] right hand of rightness and justice.

ISAIAH 41:10

What does this Scripture mean when it says, "I will strengthen and harden you to difficulties"? It means God makes you stronger and stronger as you go through things. It also means you become less affected by the difficulties and challenges you face as time goes on. It is like exercise; when you first do it, you get sore, but as you press through the soreness, you build muscle and gain strength and soon find ease in doing what was once very difficult.

As you have been walking with God, He has been strengthening you. You can face each new challenge, overcoming any fears; God will continually give you the strength you need to overcome, and you will grow in maturity.

Power Thought: Every challenge I face is an opportunity for God to strengthen me.

Encourage One Another

Therefore encourage (admonish, exhort) one another and edify
(strengthen and build up) one another, just as you are doing.
                                        1 THESSALONIANS 5:11

Words of encouragement build people up and strengthen them to
be all they can be in life. They help people not to give up on their
dreams, but to press on until they have victory.

Many of the world's great inventions came through people who
had to resist believing the discouraging words spoken to them by
others. Thankfully, they didn't give up; but how many great things
have we missed because people got discouraged? Probably more
than we can imagine.

Absolutely anyone can make a commitment to encourage other
people. All you have to do is ask God to use you, then begin to
see people the way He does. He sees the good in people, and you
can train yourself to do the same thing. Look for the positive and
magnify it! Ask God to put encouraging things in your heart that
you can speak to others.

Power Thought: I choose to encourage and refuse to be
discouraged.

Why Does God Wait?

Is anything too hard or too wonderful for the Lord? At the appointed time, when the season [for her delivery] comes around, I will return to you and Sarah shall have borne a son.

GENESIS 18:14

When God came to Abraham and told him He was going to bless him, Abraham told God that he wanted a son (see Genesis 15:2). What he had asked for was impossible in the natural due to his wife's old age. She was past the age of childbearing, but all things are possible with God. God delights in us when we come to Him with our requests, and nothing is too hard for Him.

Sometimes when we ask God for something He doesn't answer us right away, and in Abraham's case, it was twenty years before he saw the fulfillment of God's promise to him. God often waits on things and we don't understand why, but we can and should continue to trust Him and His timing in our lives.

Power Thought: I trust God's perfect timing and believe that nothing is too hard for Him.

The Fullness of God

[That you may really come] to know [practically, through experience for yourselves] the love of Christ, which far surpasses mere knowledge [without experience]; that you may be filled [through all your being] unto all the fullness of God [may have the richest measure of the divine Presence, and become a body wholly filled and flooded with God Himself]!

EPHESIANS 3:19

Does God want us to be full of ourselves? No! According to this Scripture, we are supposed to be full of God! We should get ourselves off of our minds and fill our minds instead with the "fullness of God." Let your mind and mouth and your entire body be "flooded with God Himself!" We can do this by thinking about Him, talking about Him, and letting our actions glorify Him.

Pray as David did in Psalm 27:4: "One thing have I asked of the Lord, that will I seek, inquire for, and [insistently] require: that I may dwell in the house of the Lord [in His presence] all the days of my life." The one thing David wanted was: God!

Power Thought: I am full of God, not myself.

Hold Fast Your Confession

*Inasmuch then as we have a great High Priest Who has
[already] ascended and passed through the heavens, Jesus the
Son of God, let us hold fast our confession [of faith in Him].*

HEBREWS 4:14

Hebrews 4:14 and 10:23 both tell us to hold fast our confession of
faith in Christ. When we hold fast to something, it indicates something or someone might be trying to take it away from us.

Satan will try to steal our confession by putting wrong thoughts
in our minds, hoping the thoughts will produce wrong words that
will come out of our mouths and then create wrong actions—
Satan fights anything that will produce good results in our lives.
To *confess* means "to agree with, or say the same thing." Begin saying the same things God says, and get into agreement with Him so
His good plan for your life can come to pass. Hold on to your right
confession even when circumstances don't look good, because
they will change!

Power Thought: I will hold fast to my confession of faith;
I agree with God and His promises for my life.

Blameless before God

Even as [in His love] He chose us [actually picked us out for Himself as His own] in Christ before the foundation of the world, that we should be holy (consecrated and set apart for Him) and blameless in His sight, even above reproach, before Him in love.   EPHESIANS 1:4

Not only does God love us, but He chooses to view us as being right with Him, accepted and blameless. This is our inherited position with God because of faith in Jesus; it is not based on our own works of right or wrong, but entirely on faith.

God wants us to learn proper behavior, but He accepts and loves us first. Then once we are rooted and grounded in the knowledge of His unconditional love, He can begin the work of transforming our characters into the image of His Son.

Power Thought: I am chosen by Christ, and in Him I am blameless before God.

Be Thankful at All Times

I will bless the Lord at all times; His praise shall continually be in my mouth.

PSALM 34:1

Some people are very thankful for every little thing that is done for them, while others are never satisfied, no matter how much is done on their behalf. Choose to be a grateful person—one filled with gratitude not only toward God, but also toward people. When someone does something nice for you, let that person know you appreciate it.

Meditate daily on all the things you have to be thankful for. Speak them to the Lord in prayer, and as you do, you will find your heart filling up with His peace, love, and joy. I believe thankful people are happy people, so go ahead and increase your joy today by being thankful.

Power Thought: I am a grateful person and continually praise God with my mouth.

His Peace, My Responsibility

Peace I leave with you; My [own] peace I now give and bequeath to you. Not as the world gives do I give to you. Do not let your hearts be troubled, neither let them be afraid. [Stop allowing yourselves to be agitated and disturbed; and do not permit yourselves to be fearful and intimidated and cowardly and unsettled.]   JOHN 14:27

Perhaps you have never thought about how important it is to manage your emotions. I imagine we all think, *I can't help how I act when I am having a hard time.* That is a normal human reaction, but with God on your side helping you, you don't have to behave the way a "normal" person would.

It is obvious from Jesus' words in John 14:27 that He desires for you to have wonderful peace, but please notice He is also giving you a responsibility. He wants you to choose to control the negative emotions that can steal your peace. You cannot always control your circumstances, but you can control yourself with God's help.

Power Thought: God has given me His peace, and I will walk in it.

Undeveloped Fruit

I am the Vine; you are the branches. Whoever lives in Me and I in him bears much (abundant) fruit.

JOHN 15:5

Have you ever responded unbecomingly to a situation (with anger or impatience, for example) and thought, *Who is this person? I thought I was nice and sweet!* Sometimes we think we already have the fruit of the Spirit fully developed in us simply because we are Christians (see Galatians 5:22–23). But when we are caught off guard, or our fruit is "squeezed," we find out just how undeveloped the fruit in us actually is. These incidents are tests that are actually very good for us because they help us know the areas where we are weak and still need to grow.

The more you practice displaying the fruit of self-control in your thoughts, words, and actions, the riper the fruit will become. I encourage you to depend on God's grace (undeserved favor and blessing) to work through you to produce the fruit needed. If we "try" outside of Him, we will fail, but when we partner with Him, we see His will come to pass. Stay attached to the Vine (see John 15), and your fruit will appear at the right time.

Power Thought: I have self-control over my thoughts, words, and actions.

Do Not Complain—Be Thankful!

Do everything without complaining or arguing.
PHILIPPIANS 2:14 NIV

One of the reasons the Israelites spent forty years wandering in the wilderness for what should have been an eleven-day journey was because they were complaining.

"And the people spoke against God and against Moses, Why have you brought us out of Egypt to die in the wilderness? For there is no bread, neither is there any water, and we loathe this light (contemptible, unsubstantial) manna" (Numbers 21:5). Do you hear their bad attitude? They believe their discomfort is God's fault! Or Moses' fault! And they are complaining about the *miraculous* manna God sent *daily* from heaven to feed them!

One of the worst parts about complaining is that it prevents us from seeing all the blessings we do have. Do you have a situation or circumstance you want to be free from? Start finding things to be thankful for. Don't focus on the things you don't have, but look at all you do have in Christ.

Power Thought: I am thankful at all times for everything I have in Christ.

See Yourself the Way God Sees You

Before I formed you in the womb I knew [and] approved of
you [as My chosen instrument], and before you were born
I separated and set you apart, consecrating you; [and] I
appointed you as a prophet to the nations.

JEREMIAH 1:5

Take comfort in knowing that God knew all about you even before you were born, and He still chose to be in relationship with you. How you think God views you and how you feel about yourself on the inside determines the quality of life you will have.

It's important to ask yourself what kind of relationship you have with *you*. Do you enjoy spending time alone? Are you able to forgive yourself (receive God's forgiveness) when you make mistakes? Are you patient with yourself while God is changing you? Are you able to freely be the precious individual God created you to be?

When you ask these questions and answer them honestly, you can begin to understand what kind of relationship you have with yourself. If you can relax about yourself, then you can usually relax about life in general.

Power Thought: Because God loves and approves of me, I can have a healthy relationship with myself.

You Have All the Faith You Need

Then the disciples came to Jesus and asked privately, Why
could we not drive [the demon] out? He said to them, Because
of the littleness of your faith [that is, your lack of firmly relying
trust]. For truly I say to you, if you have faith [that is living]
like a grain of mustard seed, you can say to this mountain,
Move from here to yonder place, and it will move; and nothing
will be impossible to you.   MATTHEW 17:19–20

I sometimes hear people say, "I just don't have enough faith for
that." The truth is we all have the faith we need to do whatever
God's will is for us, but the key to success is where we place that
faith. If you put your faith in yourself or in other people, you will
be disappointed. But if you put it in God, you will be amazed at
what He can do through you. Remember: "All things are possible
with God" (Matthew 19:26).

Power Thought: Nothing in God's will is impossible
when I have faith in Him.

More Than Conquerors

Yet amid all these things we are more than conquerors and gain a surpassing victory through Him Who loved us.

ROMANS 8:37

As Christians, we often hear people quote Romans 8:37, which says we are more than conquerors. For years, I have pondered what being "more than a conqueror" actually means.

I'm sure other people have different interpretations, but I have come to the conclusion that being "more than a conqueror" means you have such confidence that no matter what comes up in your life, you know that through Christ you can handle it. You know before you are ever faced with a problem that you're going to have victory over it. You believe you can do whatever you need to do in life. Therefore, you don't dread things, you don't fear the unknown, and you don't live in anxiety about what's going to happen. It doesn't really matter what the specifics of each situation are, you know you will be victorious through Christ.

Power Thought: I am more than a conqueror through Christ.

When Fear Comes

When I am afraid, I will trust in you.   PSALM 56:3 NIV

I have heard that there are 365 references in God's Word to "fear not"—one for every day of the year. *Fear not* means to resist fear and not let it control your actions.

The only acceptable attitude God's children can ever have toward fear is, "I will not fear." If you let fear rule in your life, it will steal your peace and joy and prevent you from fulfilling your destiny.

Are you confident in God? Do you believe right now, no matter what comes against you, victory is yours through Christ? Form a habit of saying out loud several times a day, "I will not fear." If you do, then it will be one of the first things coming out of your mouth when fear does come.

———————

Power Thought: I will not fear. I trust You, Lord.

God's Instructions on Forgiveness

But I say to you who are listening now to Me: [in order to heed, make it a practice to] love your enemies, treat well (do good to, act nobly toward) those who detest you and pursue you with hatred.   LUKE 6:27

We are commanded several times in God's Word to forgive those who abuse us or mistreat us, to pray for them and love them, and to wait for God's justice. These instructions are not easy to follow; we must make an effort to forgive and to let go of anger. If you want to know the truth, I actually feel this is one of the most difficult things God asks of us. It is hard, but not impossible. The Lord never requires us to do anything without giving us the ability to do it. We may not want to forgive, but we are able to do so with God's help. When we do forgive, we are doing ourselves a favor and saving ourselves a lot of misery.

Power Thought: I treat my enemies with forgiveness, love, and kindness.

Love Yourself

You shall love your neighbor as [you do] yourself.
                                          MATTHEW 22:39

Listening to ourselves can be quite an education. Do you say negative and unkind things about yourself? If you do, it is because deep in your heart, you have a bad attitude about yourself, and it will affect all of your relationships. God doesn't want you to say bad things about yourself; He wants you to love and respect yourself so you can love and respect others. You cannot give away what you don't have in you already.

God loves us unconditionally, and since God, Who is perfect, loves us, then surely we can love ourselves. We all make mistakes and want to change, and we should work with the Holy Spirit toward those changes, but through Christ we can love and value ourselves even while we are imperfect. The better you get along with yourself, the better you will get along with others.

Power Thought: I receive God's love for me, and I love others as I do myself.

God Is Faithful

God is faithful (reliable, trustworthy, and therefore ever true to His promise, and He can be depended on); by Him you were called into companionship and participation with His Son, Jesus Christ our Lord.   1 CORINTHIANS 1:9

Worry is failing to trust God to take care of the various situations in our lives. When we worry, we are actually acting on the thought *If I try hard enough, I can find a solution to my problem*, which is the opposite of trusting God.

Most of us have spent our lives trying to take care of ourselves, and it takes time to learn how to trust God in every situation. But we learn by doing. We have to step out in faith, and as we do, we will experience the faithfulness of God, which makes it easier to trust Him the next time.

Power Thought: I trust God's faithfulness.

You Have Not Passed This Way Before

Yet a space must be kept between you and it, about 2,000 cubits by measure; come not near it, that you may [be able to see the ark and] know the way you must go, for you have not passed this way before.   JOSHUA 3:4

Pay particular attention to these words in the Scripture above: "you have not passed this way before." Whether it is a job, a place to live, a relationship, an addition to your family, a position of influence, an exercise program, a church, a hobby, or a way of serving your community—if you have "not passed this way before," it is new to you. You may not know how to get there or what to do when you arrive, but if you follow God, you will arrive at your destination and He will direct you in everything you need to do. You have no need to be afraid of new things because God is always with you and He will never leave you. Be courageous and trust Him to help you.

Power Thought: When God leads me into a new situation, I trust Him to provide everything I need.

Be Like God

Therefore be imitators of God [copy Him and follow His example], as well-beloved children [imitate their father].

EPHESIANS 5:1

We are taught in this Scripture to be imitators of God. So however God is, that is the way we should desire to be. God sees the desires of our hearts and will help us become more and more like Him in our behaviors.

Do you think God is sitting in the heavens today angry and crying and depressed? No, that is not God's nature. God is joyful, and He is strong; therefore, we should imitate Him.

God is also merciful and slow to anger (see Psalm 103:8). If you become angry at people over an injustice, one way to get over it is to imitate God and choose to give them mercy—forgive them even if you don't think they deserve it.

You and I can become more and more like God because His power and character are in us (see 2 Peter 1:3–4). Begin to imitate God in your life, doing what you believe He would do in situations, instead of what you feel like doing.

Power Thought: By God's grace and through His power, I imitate Him. He is my example for how to live my life.

The Pen and the Tablet

Let not mercy and kindness [shutting out all hatred and selfishness] and truth [shutting out all deliberate hypocrisy or falsehood] forsake you; bind them about your neck, write them upon the tablet of your heart. PROVERBS 3:3

In Psalm 45:1, the psalmist said his tongue was "like the pen of a ready writer." And in Proverbs 3:1–3, the Word states you should not forget God's laws but "write them upon the tablet of your heart." We see from these two Scriptures that the heart is the tablet and the tongue is the pen.

When you confess God's Word out loud with your tongue, you are effectively writing it on your heart. When you write it on your heart, it becomes more firmly established both in your heart and in the Earth. God's Word is forever "settled in heaven" (see Psalm 119:89), and we establish it in the Earth each time we speak it. When your mouth is filled with God's Word, it is a weapon against the devil . . . use it!

Power Thought: My tongue is my pen, and my heart a tablet. When I speak the Word of God, it establishes His laws on my heart.

It's a Matter of Focus

Lean on, trust in, and be confident in the Lord with all
your heart and mind and do not rely on your own insight or
understanding.   PROVERBS 3:5

When we worry, we focus on our problems. When we are anxious about things, we talk about them incessantly. Why? Because what is in our hearts eventually comes out of our mouths (see Matthew 12:34). The more we think and talk about our problems, the larger they become. Instead of meditating on the problems, we can meditate on the faithfulness of God and remind ourselves there is no need to worry.

I have heard many people say, "I just can't help it, I am a worrier." The truth is they choose to worry because they do not know how to trust God. We become good at worrying because we practice it; therefore, we can become good at trusting God if we practice. Let your first response in any situation be to trust God.

Power Thought: I trust God with all my heart and all my mind.

Say Something Good or Don't Say Anything at All

A wholesome tongue is a tree of life: but perverseness therein is a breach in the spirit. PROVERBS 15:4 KJV

It would be a wonderful world to live in if we all followed the rule that tells us to either say something good or don't say anything at all. Just imagine how pleasant our homes, schools, jobs, churches, and society in general would be. It might even be equivalent to heaven on Earth!

There is a simple rule you can follow to guide you in your conversation: If it is good, uplifting, wholesome, and pleasant, say all you want to; but if it is evil, negative, critical, and complaining, don't say it. What is in your heart will eventually come out of your mouth, so you cannot change what you say unless you change what you think. Ask God to change your heart so there is not even a hint of wanting to say something negative.

Power Thought: Everything I say is good, wholesome, and uplifting.

Talk Yourself into a Good Mood

A good man eats good from the fruit of his mouth.

PROVERBS 13:2

We talk a lot, and quite often pay no attention to what we are saying, let alone think seriously about the impact of our words. But if we are honest with ourselves, we may find some of our moods—good and bad—are directly linked to our conversations.

Anytime you become aware of your mood, whether you are feeling a bit gloomy or feeling cheerful and blessed, you should ask yourself: *What have I been talking about?* Soon you will begin to see how your words connect to your moods and attitudes.

Why not decide each day before you even get out of bed to ask God to help you talk about only things that benefit you and everyone who hears you? Since we have the power to make our days better, we would be foolish indeed if we didn't do it.

Power Thought: By God's grace, I think and speak positive words, reaping the benefits in my moods and attitudes.

No More Condemnation

Therefore, there is now no condemnation for those who are in Christ Jesus.   ROMANS 8:1 NIV

If you are a true believer in Jesus Christ, there is no way you could ever sin and not care. You know sin offends God, and you love God, so of course you will care. But there is a difference between caring about your sin and feeling condemned because of it.

We cannot fulfill our God-ordained purpose in life while we're trapped in guilt and condemned by our feelings. God doesn't want us to beat ourselves up for every mistake we make. We need to learn how to apply the work of the cross in our lives, accepting by faith that Jesus shed His blood to forgive our sins, receiving His forgiveness, and going on to do the things God has called us to do without a trace of guilt. This may be a new way of thinking for you, but it is biblical, and it is your right as a believer in Jesus Christ.

Power Thought: I am human, and I make mistakes; yet by the grace of God, I am free from condemnation.

Lift Up Your Eyes

I lift up my eyes to the hills—where does my help come from?
My help comes from the LORD, the Maker of heaven and earth.

PSALM 121:1–2 NIV

One of the ways God taught me to deal with the past is to confess His promises instead of talk about how I feel. We all have painful issues from the past we must grapple with. Perhaps you were teased mercilessly as a child and still feel insecure or sensitive because of that old pain. Maybe someone you loved left you without explanation. Whatever the source of your pain, always remember that God loves you.

You don't have to spend your life mourning over something you can't do anything about. God wants to heal and restore every hurt, injustice, and mistake in your life. God will help you. . . . He's waiting to help you.

Power Thought: My help comes from the Lord.

Listen for the Still, Small Voice

For what person perceives (knows and understands) what
passes through a man's thoughts except the man's own spirit
within him? Just so no one discerns (comes to know and
comprehend) the thoughts of God except the Spirit of God.

1 CORINTHIANS 2:11

The Holy Spirit dwells in us, and He knows the mind of God. The Holy Spirit is our Teacher, and one of His purposes is to reveal to us God's wisdom and revelation.

While the Holy Spirit wants to enlighten our minds, all too often we miss what the Spirit is attempting to reveal because our human thoughts are shouting too loud. The mind should not be filled with reasoning, worry, anxiety, fear, and the like. It should be calm, quiet, and serene.

The ways of the Holy Spirit are gentle; most of the time He speaks to us in a "still small voice" (1 Kings 19:12 KJV). So it is vital that we learn to keep ourselves in a condition conducive to hearing God's divine revelation.

Power Thought: I hear the still, small voice of the Holy Spirit, and I follow His wisdom.

Do Things God's Way

[Jesus] said to Simon, "Launch out into the deep and let down your nets for a catch."

But Simon answered and said to Him, "Master, we have toiled all night and caught nothing; nevertheless at Your word I will let down the net." And when they had done this, they caught a great number of fish, and their net was breaking.

LUKE 5:4–6 NKJV, emphasis added

In the Scripture above, after a long night of not catching any fish, Jesus tells Peter to try one more time. What Jesus told Peter to do probably didn't make any sense to him, and I doubt that he *felt* like doing it, but he did what the Lord said, and he received what was probably the biggest catch of his fishing career.

Being led by *your* thoughts, feelings, and emotions won't bring in a big catch.

But you can do what God says, when He says it, whether it makes any sense to you or not, and your blessings will amaze you.

Power Thought: Even if it doesn't make sense to me, I will trust and obey God.

God Wants You to Enjoy Your Life

There is nothing better for a man than that he should eat and drink and make himself enjoy good in his labor. Even this, I have seen, is from the hand of God.

ECCLESIASTES 2:24

In this Scripture, King Solomon, who is considered to have been very wise, said you are to make yourself enjoy the good of your labor. That sounds as if it is something you must choose to do on purpose. You can learn to enjoy all of life, even things others would consider ordinary and boring.

Many people have the mentality of just trying to "endure" large portions of their lives, but I believe it is tragic to live and not enjoy every moment. I admit some things are more emotionally pleasant than others, but you can learn to enjoy God's presence in everything you do. Try repeating internally throughout the day to yourself: *God is with me, and the moment I have right now is a gift from Him.*

_____

Power Thought: I enjoy each moment God has given me.

Content and Stable in All Circumstances

I have learned how to be content (satisfied to the point where I am not disturbed or disquieted) in whatever state I am.

PHILIPPIANS 4:11

Stability and contentment enable us to enjoy our lives. I have discovered I like myself better when I am stable and content, and I think other people like me better this way too. I believe the same is true for you. Becoming emotionally stable and content is very important to a powerful life, and as you grow in these qualities, you'll find yourself strengthened as never before.

Paul said he *learned* how to be content in all circumstances. Likewise, you will have to learn in this area and begin believing you can be content and stable before you actually see the fruit of it in your life. God's Word states that we can and should speak of nonexistent things as if they already existed (see Romans 4:17). Begin to think and say you are content and emotionally stable, and it will help you become that way.

Power Thought: I am content and stable in all circumstances.

Confusion Is Not from God

For God is not the author of confusion, but of peace, as in all churches of the saints. 1 CORINTHIANS 14:33 KJV

There is nothing wrong with pondering some things in our hearts, as Mary did when the angel of the Lord told her she would give birth to the promised Messiah (see Luke 2:19). Many times it is while we are pondering or meditating on something that God gives us revelation or understanding. It is one thing to ponder, but another thing to worry.

When we are pondering, in a sense we are praying, "Lord, I don't know what this means. I don't really understand it. I need some direction." However, when we are worrying, we are trying to figure things out on our own, and we often end up confused about what to do. As soon as you become confused, you have stopped pondering and started worrying and reasoning. Seek after peace, not confusion, because God is not the author of confusion.

Power Thought: It is God's will for me to have peace and not confusion.

Free from Judgment

I care very little if I am judged by you or by any human court;
indeed, I do not even judge myself.

1 CORINTHIANS 4:3 NIV

Paul was confident in Christ. Because he knew he was made acceptable to God in Christ (see Romans 5:19), he accepted himself. He
did not judge himself or receive judgment from other people.

Paul had persecuted Christians prior to God opening his eyes
to the truth. He said he had to make an effort to let go of the past
and press on toward perfection. He also clarified that he did not
think he had arrived (see Philippians 3:12–14). In other words,
Paul did not claim perfection, but neither did he have a bad attitude toward himself. He knew he made mistakes, but he did not
reject and despise himself because of them.

The type of confidence we see displayed by Paul is very freeing;
it reminds us that Jesus died so we could be free (see John 8:36).

Power Thought: I am free from human judgment because
of who I am in Christ.

What's in Your Hand?

And the Lord said to him, What is that in your hand? And he said, A rod. EXODUS 4:2

In Exodus, God appeared to Moses to tell him to lead the Israelites out of Egypt, but Moses didn't believe he could do all God was asking him to do. God responded to Moses' excuses by asking him, "What is that in your hand?"

God is essentially saying, "Stop telling Me what you don't have and can't do, and tell Me what you *do* have—what is in your hand?" Then God takes what Moses has—a rod (stick)—and fills it with His power.

God can use anything we are willing to offer Him. If He can use a stick, surely He can use you and me! Don't wait until you can figure out how to do it all on your own—let God infuse His power into you *now* and do whatever He asks of you through His strength.

Power Thought: When I give God what I do have, He will do great things through me.

Listening to God

This is what the LORD says—your Redeemer, the Holy One of Israel: "I am the LORD your God, who teaches you what is best for you, who directs you in the way you should go."

ISAIAH 48:17 NIV

God wants to give us direction, but we need to learn to listen in order for that to happen. God leads us in many different ways. Some of the most frequent are His Word, peace, and wisdom. But God cannot lead us at all if we are not willing to do whatever He shows us to do, even if it is not what we would prefer.

Are you ready and willing to say, "Lord, if You lead me, I will follow"? If you make that commitment and truly mean it, then you can expect God's guidance in your life. It may not always come immediately when you ask for it, but it will come. While you are waiting, just continue to thank Him that He has a plan and will reveal it to you at the right time.

Power Thought: I listen to God, and He leads me every day, in every situation in my life.

Come Clean

If we confess our sins, he is faithful and just and will forgive us our sins and purify us from all unrighteousness.

1 JOHN 1:9 NIV

Peace with God is maintained by never attempting to hide sin. We must always come clean with God and keep good communication open between us. God is not surprised by our weaknesses and failures; actually, He knew about the mistakes we would make before we made them. All we need to do is admit them and repent of them, and He is faithful to forgive us continually from all sin.

It is important to do the best you can out of your love for God, but since none of us are perfect, we will make mistakes. When we do, we can talk openly to our Father about them and maintain a relationship of peace with Him. When you need cleansing, don't ever run from God, but run to Him!

Power Thought: I am at peace with God because I don't try to hide my mistakes from Him.

How to Have Great Faith

Looking away [from all that will distract] to Jesus, Who is the Leader and the Source of our faith [giving the first incentive for our belief] and is also its Finisher [bringing it to maturity and perfection].   HEBREWS 12:2

Hebrews 12:2 instructs us to look away from all that distracts us and focus on Jesus, Who is the Leader and Source of our faith. If we look to God, think about Him, and speak of His goodness instead of focusing on our problems, then we focus on faith. As we focus on faith, it grows and grows.

Little faith can become great faith as you use it more often. When you take steps to trust God, you will experience His faithfulness, and, in turn, you'll be encouraged to have even greater faith. As your faith develops and grows, your problems will have less power over you and you will worry less.

Power Thought: Jesus, the Author and Finisher of my faith, is my Source of strength.

Overcoming the Wandering Mind

Keep your foot [give your mind to what you are doing] when
you go [as Jacob to sacred Bethel] to the house of God.

                                                    ECCLESIASTES 5:1

Even though a person attends church, the enemy knows very well
if that person can't keep his mind on what is being taught, he will
gain absolutely nothing by being there.

Satan wants you to think you are mentally deficient—that
something is wrong with you, causing you not to be able to focus.
But the truth is you just need to discipline your mind. Don't let it
run all over the place, doing whatever it pleases. Begin today to
"keep your foot," to keep your mind on what you're doing. Forming any new habit takes time, effort, and a lot of help from God,
but it can be done and it is worth it in the end.

Power Thought: I am able to keep my mind on track and
focus on what I am doing.

Adding Value to Others

But encourage one another daily, as long as it is called Today,
so that none of you may be hardened by sin's deceitfulness.

HEBREWS 3:13 NIV

There are people who are gifted by God with a special ability to encourage others (see Romans 12:6–8). However, even if encouraging others is not a gift you particularly have, you are still responsible to do it. God's Word teaches us that we are to encourage one another *daily*!

We have been entrusted with a great power. When we encourage others, it builds them up and makes them strong (see 1 Thessalonians 5:11). However, without that encouragement they might become weary and give up on something they need to finish.

God is "[the Source] of every comfort (consolation and encouragement)" (2 Corinthians 1:3). Since God is an encourager, we should be the same way. Anytime you do what God does, you can be assured you are doing the things that are right and that will produce joy, peace, and power for your life.

Power Thought: Today I will encourage and add value to everyone I meet.

Your Thoughts Are Not Hidden from God

*Search me [thoroughly], O God, and know my heart! Try me
and know my thoughts! And see if there is any wicked or hurtful
way in me, and lead me in the way everlasting.*

PSALM 139:23–24

What if your mind were a movie screen and everyone could see
what you were thinking? Most of us have thoughts we wouldn't
want anyone else to see. But shouldn't we grow to the point where
we wouldn't be ashamed for anybody to see what we were thinking? Shouldn't that be our goal?

The Bible says the degree of God's glory (His excellence displayed) in us can change. Our thought lives can change little by
little as God changes us from one degree of glory to another (see
2 Corinthians 3:18). Work with Him to cultivate a thought life you
wouldn't be ashamed for anyone to see!

Power Thought: My thoughts are not hidden from God. I
know I can change with His help.

Practice Makes Perfect

*Make me understand the way of Your precepts; so shall I
meditate on and talk of Your wondrous works.*

PSALM 119:27

Mark 4:24 says the amount of time you give to the Word will
determine the amount of knowledge and virtue that comes back to
you. As humans, we can be rather lazy, and many people want to
get something for nothing (with no effort on their part); however,
according to this Scripture, that is not the way it works.

If you want to do what the Word of God says and tap into the
full power available to you, you will have to spend time reading
the Word, meditating on it, pondering and contemplating it, talking about it, and rehearsing and practicing it in your thinking.

Remember the old saying "Practice makes perfect"? We don't
expect to be experts at other things in life without a lot of study, so
why would we expect living the Christian life to be any different?

Power Thought: I study the Word of God so I can learn
God's ways.

Shake It Off

And whoever will not receive and accept and welcome you nor listen to your message, as you leave that house or town, shake the dust [of it] from your feet.   MATTHEW 10:14

Jesus gave instructions to His disciples regarding how to handle rejection. He told them to "shake it off." Basically He was saying, "Don't let it bother you. Don't let it keep you from doing what I have called you to do."

Jesus was despised and rejected (see Isaiah 53:3), and yet He never seemed to let it bother Him. I am sure He felt pain just as you and I do when we experience rejection, but He did not let it prevent Him from fulfilling His purpose.

Jesus told His disciples not to be concerned about rejection because, in reality, people who rejected them were really rejecting Jesus (see Luke 10:16). Why should you concern yourself with the opinions of people? You cannot control what they think, so leave them and their opinions in God's hands and focus on doing God's will.

Power Thought: I don't let rejection bother me because I have the only approval that matters: God's.

Be an Example

*But now I write to you not to associate with anyone who bears
the name of [Christian] brother if he is known to be guilty of
immorality or greed, or is an idolater [whose soul is devoted
to any object that usurps the place of God], or is a person with
a foul tongue [railing, abusing, reviling, slandering], or is a
drunkard or a swindler or a robber. [No] you must not so much
as eat with such a person.*   1 CORINTHIANS 5:11

The apostle Paul told the Corinthians not to associate with a
believer who had a foul tongue, which included gossiping and criti-
cizing. In order to be a good example to people who are sinning,
you must be careful not to do the negative things they do or to say
the hurtful things they say. You don't want to give the impression
that you think you are better than they are, but you must lovingly,
humbly, and gently decline to be involved in conversation and in
other behaviors you know are displeasing to God.

Don't be passive and let other people infect you with their bad
attitudes and evil conversation, but instead make a decision to be
a good influence on them.

Power Thought: I will not gossip, criticize, or spread
rumors about others.

Conforming to Righteousness

*For being ignorant of the righteousness that God ascribes
[which makes one acceptable to Him in word, thought, and
deed] and seeking to establish a righteousness (a means of
salvation) of their own, they did not obey or submit themselves
to God's righteousness.*   ROMANS 10:3

Righteousness means being made right with God and then consistently conforming to His will in thought, word, and deed. In other
words, when we are made right with God, we begin to think right,
talk right, and act right. It is a *process* in which we are continually making progress. We may have setbacks, but overall we move
forward.

The Holy Spirit works in us, helping us become the fullness
of what the Father wants us to be in Christ. The outworking of
righteousness—which is ultimately seen in right thoughts, words,
and actions—cannot begin until we accept and believe in our
right standing with God through Jesus Christ.

Power Thought: My thoughts, words, and actions are
acceptable to God because Christ lives in me.

Agree with God

Again I tell you, if two of you on earth agree (harmonize together, make a symphony together) about whatever [anything and everything] they may ask, it will come to pass and be done for them by My Father in heaven.   MATTHEW 18:19

Not only does God have a plan for your life, but the devil has a plan for you too. Satan wants you to agree with him because the Bible says when people come into agreement, power increases.

When the devil tries to tell you that you don't have any future and you've made too many mistakes, you need to say, "God is the God of a second chance. And I not only have a future, but I've got a good future. God is going to do great things in my life." If the devil can get you to agree with him, you will have what he wants you to have, but if you stay in agreement with God, then you'll have what God wants you to have. Who are you going to agree with?

Power Thought: I agree with God.

Meditate on the Word of God

I will meditate on Your precepts and have respect to Your ways
[the paths of life marked out by Your law].   PSALM 119:15

The Word of God teaches us what we should spend our time thinking about. The psalmist said he thought about or meditated on the
"precepts" of God. That means he spent a lot of time pondering
and thinking on the ways of God, His instructions, and His teachings. Psalm 1:3 says the person who does this "shall be like a tree
firmly planted [and tended] by the streams of water, ready to bring
forth its fruit in its season; its leaf also shall not fade or wither;
and everything he does shall prosper [and come to maturity]."

It is very beneficial to think about God's Word because it
reveals His will and His amazing plan for His children. The more
time you spend meditating on the Word, the more your joy will
increase and you will bear good fruit.

––––––––––––––––

Power Thought: I will always meditate on the Word of
God and His precepts.

The Power of Position

And the leaders of the church had nothing to add to what I was preaching. (By the way, their reputation as great leaders made no difference to me, for God has no favorites.)

GALATIANS 2:6 NLT

Don't let your value become attached to a position of power or authority. Positions can come and go in life, but God and His love for you remain. Our worth and value, our acceptance and approval, come from Him. As long as we have Him, we have the most valuable thing in the world.

When we need what the world offers in order to feel good about ourselves, God often withholds it. Once we no longer *need* those things, He can give them to us because He knows they will not control us. You may have friends, influence, position, authority, acceptance, etc., but the key to keeping them is knowing beyond a shadow of doubt you don't need to have them to be happy and fulfilled.

Power Thought: My value comes from who I am in Christ.

Jesus Is the Truth

I am the Way and the Truth and the Life; no one comes to the Father except by (through) Me. JOHN 14:6

When we believe lies from Satan or other people, we end up in bondage, but the truth of God's Word makes us free when we believe it. God's Word brings light into our lives and dispels the darkness. Continue in God's Word and you will experience many breakthroughs and freedoms in your life. I know it is true because I have experienced it myself.

Jesus is the Truth, and when we believe what He says and believe in the way He teaches, then we will have the lives that He planned for us. The quality of life God offers us is life as He is living it. Just imagine: we can share in the life of God by simply learning truth and applying it in our lives.

Power Thought: Jesus is the Way, the Truth, and the Life!

Develop God's Nature in You

No one born (begotten) of God [deliberately, knowingly, and
habitually] practices sin, for God's nature abides in him
[His principle of life, the divine sperm, remains permanently
within him]; and he cannot practice sinning because he is born
(begotten) of God.　　　　　　　　　　　　　　1 JOHN 3:9

According to this Scripture, when we are born again, we cannot
continue to purposefully, willfully, knowingly sin. Yet Paul says in
Romans 7:15, "I want to do what is right, but I don't do it. Instead,
I do what I hate" (NLT). Paul, like the rest of us, was growing into
the fullness of what was his in Christ.

We can get confused when we read in the Word that we have
the mind of Christ (see 1 Corinthians 2:16) and the fruit of the
Spirit (see Galatians 5:22–23), but we aren't experiencing them
in our lives. It is important to understand that having the mind of
Christ doesn't mean you automatically think as Christ thinks, and
having God's seeds of love, joy, and peace in you doesn't mean you
automatically operate in them.

When a woman first becomes pregnant, no one can tell because
the seed egg has to grow. Similarly, when God blesses us with His
nature, or the seed of all that He is, we have to let it develop before
we see it fully take effect in our lives. Be patient, God is working
in you.

Power Thought: God's nature is developing in me.

Active Faith

Recalling unceasingly before our God and Father your work energized by faith and service motivated by love and unwavering hope in [the return of] our Lord Jesus Christ (the Messiah).   1 THESSALONIANS 1:3

God's Word encourages us to have an active faith, and by doing so we shut the door to laziness, procrastination, and passivity. You are more powerful than you may realize. God has given you free will, and that means you can decide to act on, think, and speak what is right, and nothing can stop you.

It takes time to train yourself to think, speak, and act positively, and you may not succeed every day. If you realize you have failed, don't waste time being discouraged; just pick up where you left off and begin again. Be kind to yourself because beating yourself up for every mistake is just the result of another negative thought that needs to be eliminated.

When you decide to act in favor of God's ways, He always joins forces with you for assured victory.

Power Thought: My faith in God is alive and active; I have an active faith.

What about Me?

Whoever does not love does not know God, because God is love.
1 JOHN 4:8 NIV

God is love, and His nature is that of a giver. He gives, He helps, He cares, and He sacrifices. He does not do these things occasionally; they represent His constant attitude toward us. Love is not something God does—it is Who He is. He always offers us love, generosity, grace, and help. God does chastise His children when they need it, but He even does that out of love and for our own good to teach us the right way to live.

Everything God does is for our good; all of His commands are intended to help us have the best lives we can possibly have. Because God's love has been poured out in our hearts by the Holy Spirit (see Romans 5:5), we can love and be kind to others, which means taking the focus off of ourselves, silencing the internal voice that asks, *What about me?*, and learning to follow Jesus' example of being kind, generous, and loving toward others.

Power Thought: I love because I know God, and God is love.

Overcome Rejection

Didn't you ever read this in the Scriptures? "The stone that the builders rejected has now become the cornerstone. This is the LORD's doing, and it is wonderful to see."

MARK 12:10–11 NLT

We all fear earthly rejection too much. Jesus was rejected, and He survived. You can too! When I say you will survive, I don't mean you will just barely make it; I mean rejection will not leave you brokenhearted, and it will not stop you from doing what God wants you to do. No one enjoys being rejected, but we can experience it and still be victorious.

We are not responsible for our reputations; God is! So relax and keep thinking to yourself, *I may not be accepted by everyone, but I am accepted and loved by God.* Repeat it over and over until you believe it and are no longer bothered if people reject you.

If you have God, you have all you need. If He knows you need anything else, He will provide that also (see Matthew 6:8, 33–34). If you value the unconditional love of God more than the conditional approval of people, you will overcome rejection.

Power Thought: I can overcome rejection because I have received God's love.

Speaking Right Words

A man's [moral] self shall be filled with the fruit of his mouth;
and with the consequence of his words he must be satisfied
[whether good or evil].   PROVERBS 18:20

Words are wonderful when used with good intentions. They can encourage, edify, and give confidence. When we understand the power of words and realize we can choose what we think and speak, our lives can be transformed. Our words are not forced on us—they formulate in our thoughts and then we speak them. We can learn to choose our thoughts, to resist wrong ones, and think on good, healthy, right ones.

When you get up in the morning, if there is something you need to attend to that you're not looking forward to, you can say, "I dread this day," or you can say, "God will give me strength today to do whatever I need to do and to do it with joy."

Power Thought: With God's help, I choose to speak right words, and it increases my joy.

Living Ordinary Days with an Extraordinary Attitude

This is the day which the Lord has brought about; we will rejoice and be glad in it. PSALM 118:24

I believe the psalmist discovered the secret to living ordinary days with extraordinary enthusiasm. He simply decided and declared that since the Lord had made each day, and that it was a gift to him, he would enjoy it and be glad. He made a decision that produced the feelings he wanted rather than waiting to see how he felt.

God's presence makes life exciting if we have a proper understanding of life as a whole. Everything we do is sacred and amazing if we do it unto the Lord and believe He is with us. Ask yourself right now if you truly believe God is with you even in the midst of very ordinary tasks. If your answer is yes, then you can have an extraordinary day!

Power Thought: I will rejoice in "ordinary" days because God is with me every day.

Liberty with Limits

You say, "I am allowed to do anything"—but not everything is good for you. And even though "I am allowed to do anything," I must not become a slave to anything.

1 CORINTHIANS 6:12 NLT

Discipline is the price of freedom; it is the door to liberation. When we are not disciplined, we become slaves; we fall under the power of things that should have no control over us.

The apostle Paul echoed a similar sentiment in 1 Corinthians 10:23 when he wrote: "All things are legitimate [permissible—and we are free to do anything we please], but not all things are helpful (expedient, profitable, and wholesome). All things are legitimate, but not all things are constructive [to character] and edifying [to spiritual life]."

Paul is saying he is technically free to do anything he wants to do, but he restrains himself from doing things that would not be wise. Making decisions based on whether or not your activity will enhance your character or help you spiritually is a wise approach to practicing discipline.

***

Power Thought: Jesus gives me discipline and self-control.

Let the Redeemed of the Lord Say So

Let the redeemed of the Lord say so, whom He has delivered from the hand of the adversary.   PSALM 107:2

The Bible says those who belong to God are redeemed and they should say so. You are redeemed! Jesus has paid the price for your redemption! It is yours, and you need to learn to agree with it!

Start declaring out loud by faith, "I am redeemed from sin, guilt, and condemnation. I am redeemed from anger, bitterness, jealousy, and fear; and I am free to love God, myself, and other people." You must get these truths into your spirit before you will experience them. Faith comes first and then manifestation. Faith is the evidence of things hoped for, the proof of things we do not see (see Hebrews 11:1). You make a confession of faith because you believe God's Word, not because you see or feel a certain thing. Choose to believe what God says, and say the same thing by faith.

Power Thought: I always speak words of faith.

Say What You Say on Purpose

Death and life are in the power of the tongue, and they who
indulge in it shall eat the fruit of it [for death or life].

PROVERBS 18:21

I strongly recommend confessing the Word of God out loud. Even
though what you confess may be the opposite of how you initially
feel, keep doing it; God's Word has inherent power to change your
feelings. God's Word also brings comfort to us and quiets our distraught emotions.

There is a time to talk and a time to keep silent. Sometimes the
best thing we can do is say nothing. When we do speak, it is wise
to be purposeful in what we say and think about our words before-
hand. If we truly believe our words are filled with life or death,
why wouldn't we choose what we say more carefully?

———————————

Power Thought: I choose my words carefully; I choose
words filled with life.

Seedtime and Harvest

For whatever a man sows, that and that only is what he will reap.

GALATIANS 6:7

We can see a tomato seed with our eyes and understand the process of planting and expecting a harvest of tomatoes. We cannot see attitudes, thoughts, or words, but they are seeds that operate in the spiritual (unseen) realm, and they also produce a harvest based on what was planted.

People who continually sow negative thoughts, attitudes, and words will produce many negative results in life. Likewise, those who sow positive, life-filled thoughts, attitudes, and words will see positive and good results.

A farmer doesn't plant a tomato seed and expect to get broccoli, and you should not plant negative-word seeds hoping to get a good harvest. Once you truly understand this principle and act accordingly, you can change your words and therefore you can change your life.

Power Thought: I expect a good harvest from the positive words that I sow.

Think Sessions

For who has known or understood the mind (the counsels and purposes) of the Lord so as to guide and instruct Him and give Him knowledge? But we have the mind of Christ (the Messiah) and do hold the thoughts (feelings and purposes) of His heart.

1 CORINTHIANS 2:16

Everyone should have daily think sessions, purposely sitting down where it is quiet, thinking in agreement with the Word of God, and speaking those thoughts out loud. You might start with one or more of these:

- This is the day the Lord has made; I will rejoice and be glad. I am looking forward to blessing people today.
- The words of my mouth and the meditation of my heart shall be acceptable to God.
- I have the mind of Christ.
- I am the righteousness of God in Christ.
- I am expecting God to do something great in my life.

Take time to actually think about what you are thinking about. Decide to think and speak on purpose every day!

Power Thought: I think on purpose; I have the mind of Christ.

Our Imperfections Don't Stop God

For though He was crucified in weakness, yet He goes on living by the power of God. And though we too are weak in Him [as He was humanly weak], yet in dealing with you [we shall show ourselves] alive and strong in [fellowship with] Him by the power of God.   2 CORINTHIANS 13:4

Although we all have weaknesses, we can still be blessed by God. Jacob was a man who had many weaknesses, and yet he pressed on with God and was determined to be blessed by Him (see Genesis 32). God likes that kind of determination. God is glorified through those who will not let their personal weaknesses stop Him from working through them. For God to work through us, we must first come face-to-face with the fact that we have weaknesses, and then we must determine not to let them bother us. Our imperfections are not going to stop God unless we let them do so. You might be weak in yourself, but you can be strong in Jesus.

Power Thought: Though I am weak, in Him I am strong.

Too Much Talk Leads to Sin

In a multitude of words transgression is not lacking, but he who restrains his lips is prudent.   PROVERBS 10:19

We all need to learn how to establish and maintain boundaries with our words. Proverbs 10:19 in the NIV states, "When words are many, sin is not absent, but he who holds his tongue is wise." In other words, people who talk a lot will often find themselves in trouble.

Because our words carry so much power, we need to learn to say only what needs to be said. Almost every time we have a problem with somebody, it's over something we have said or that person said. There may be other elements—something somebody is doing, for example—but the main cause of the argument most of the time is something that was said. If we learn to speak only what is wise and necessary, then we will have much more peace.

Power Thought: I speak words of wisdom that are filled with God's power.

Be Angry and Do Not Sin

When angry, do not sin; do not ever let your wrath (your exasperation, your fury or indignation) last until the sun goes down.
EPHESIANS 4:26

Being a person of faith does not mean you will never have negative or ungodly feelings. We *will* experience feelings that need to be dealt with, but we can always exercise our faith in God and ask Him to help us. The truth is, we can live beyond our feelings, rather than letting them control our lives.

I believe what we feel is not a sin as long as we are talking to God about it and leaning on His strength, choosing to act on His Word and not on how we feel. The Bible says be angry and do not sin (see Ephesians 4:26). That literally means you can *feel* angry about an injustice, but if you *deal* with it properly, it will not become sin.

Power Thought: With God's wisdom and strength, I can deal with anger properly so I do not sin.

A Spirit of Discipline and Self-Control

For God did not give us a spirit of timidity (of cowardice, of craven and cringing and fawning fear), but [He has given us a spirit] of power and of love and of calm and well-balanced mind and discipline and self-control.   2 TIMOTHY 1:7

Translated from the Greek language, the word *discipline* means "saving the mind or to be safe; an admonishment or calling to soundness of mind or to self-control." In other words, a person who is thinking properly with soundness of mind will have discipline in all areas of his or her life.

I believe our thoughts, words, and emotions are among the most important areas we need to discipline. A disciplined person will maintain the correct mental attitude toward issues that arise. Though difficult, it is still easier to maintain a right attitude than to regain it once it's lost. Don't let that statement pass by without thinking it over. Let me say it again: *It is much easier to maintain a right attitude than to regain it once it's lost.*

Power Thought: God has given me a spirit of discipline and self-control.

Level Your Ups and Downs

We live by faith, not by sight.　　　　2 CORINTHIANS 5:7 NIV

Feelings change from day to day, hour to hour, sometimes even moment to moment. Not only do they change, they can deceive. For example, you may feel you are not well liked, unappreciated, or even mistreated, but that doesn't mean those things are true. If you are having a "touchy" day, you might feel people are not treating you well, when in reality they are not treating you any differently than they always do.

Instead of riding the emotional roller coaster, which only exhausts us, we need to become stable, solid, steadfast, persevering, determined people. Renewing your mind to think and believe you are stable and content will help you get started. We can never enjoy any of God's promises until we believe them for ourselves. In the world we see then believe, but in God's kingdom we believe *and then* we see.

Power Thought: I live by faith, not by my feelings.

Calm in Adversity

Blessed (happy, fortunate, to be envied) is the man whom You discipline and instruct, O Lord, and teach out of Your law, that You may give him power to keep himself calm in the days of adversity.   PSALM 94:12–13

According to Exodus 13:17, "When Pharaoh let the people go, God led them *not* by way of the land of the Philistines, although that was nearer" (emphasis added). There was a shorter route, but God took the Israelites the long, hard way on purpose because they were not ready for the battles they would face. He continued to work with them during forty years of wandering, waiting for them to get to the point where they could praise Him in their adversity.

God will continue dealing with us until we learn how to stay peaceful in the storm. Nothing shows our spiritual maturity more than staying calm when our circumstances are not calm. Stability is a sign of maturity, and the more mature we are, the more God can trust us with His power and blessings.

———————

Power Thought: I have the power of God to remain calm in adversity.

Live to Please God

So, since Christ suffered in the flesh for us, for you, arm
yourselves with the same thought and purpose [patiently
to suffer rather than fail to please God]. For whoever has
suffered in the flesh [having the mind of Christ] is done with
[intentional] sin [has stopped pleasing himself and the world,
and pleases God].   1 PETER 4:1

Set your mind to please God, even if you have to suffer to do it.
In other words, determine to have the mind of Christ, Who was
willing to suffer for you. Suffering in the flesh means your flesh
is not going to like everything you have to deal with, but you can
set your mind to go through whatever God asks of you. If you set
your mind and stand firm, you will no longer walk in the flesh,
intentionally living in sin, but you will live for what God wills and
experience His righteousness, peace, joy, and victory in your life.

———————————

Power Thought: I live to please the One Who suffered for
me.

Remain Stable in Every Situation

He who dwells in the secret place of the Most High shall remain stable and fixed under the shadow of the Almighty [Whose power no foe can withstand].   PSALM 91:1

God's Word teaches us to remain stable during every storm of life. The first mistake we often make is listening to the "This is just too hard" lie. Satan is a liar, and he always puts thoughts into our minds that say we are not capable, can't, won't, and never will be able to do what God has asked of us. The devil is a glass-half-empty guy, but God always sees the glass as full and overflowing. Choose to adopt God's attitude and be an I-think-I-can person, instead of an I-think-I-can't person. If you believe you can remain stable and control your emotions even during times in which it is difficult to do so, you will find God working through your faith and enabling you to do what you believe.

Power Thought: God gives me the strength I need to remain stable in all circumstances.

Confident in Christ

When the man saw that he would not win the match, he touched Jacob's hip and wrenched it out of its socket. Then the man said, "Let me go, for the dawn is breaking!" But Jacob said, "I will not let you go unless you bless me."

GENESIS 32:25–26 NLT

Jacob was a cheater, a liar, and a swindler, but he wanted to make things right with God and his brother, Esau, whose birthright he had stolen—and he obviously had the confidence in God to wrestle with Him until he received a blessing. This is shocking to those of us who have difficulty being bold in prayer or in our approach to God. But here it is in black and white, written in God's Word— Jacob's confidence and boldness won him power with God, and God liked his confident attitude!

Ephesians 3:12 says, "Because of Christ and our faith in him, we can now come boldly and confidently into God's presence" (NLT).

Remember, your confidence isn't in yourself—it is in Christ.

Power Thought: Because of Christ and my faith in Him, I can come boldly, confidently, and freely into His presence.

What about Me?

If anyone intends to come after Me, let him deny himself [forget, ignore, disown, and lose sight of himself and his own interests] and take up his cross, and . . . follow with Me.

MARK 8:34

As busy people who carry overwhelming responsibilities, it is easy for our needs to be put on hold. After a while we get tired and burned-out, and the devil begins planting thoughts like *Well, what about me? Does anyone care about my needs?* Unless you know how to strike a balance between meeting your valid needs and meeting other people's needs, you can quickly fall into the trap of self-pity, thinking about "poor me" all the time, which is not a place God wants you to be. That's why you also need to rest and have enjoyment in life so you don't become worn-out and bitter.

Jesus gave His life for others, and He wants you to do the same. In fact, true joy comes only from giving your life away—not from striving to keep it (see Romans 15:2).

Power Thought: I live for God and give Him my life so I can be a blessing to others.

Forgive and Your Prayers Will Be Answered

And when you stand praying, if you hold anything against anyone, forgive him, so that your Father in heaven may forgive you your sins.　　　　　　　　　　MARK 11:25 NIV

If you are praying for a miracle or for God to bring something into your life and you aren't getting it, ask yourself if there is someone you need to forgive. Don't try to justify your anger and unforgiveness. Don't complain about your circumstances or what people have done to you; instead, trust God to be your Vindicator and have a loving attitude toward everyone.

When you pray, say to God: *God, I don't want to have any unforgiveness or anger in my heart toward anyone, so if I do, please reveal it to me so I can pray for them instead of being angry. I'm not mad at anyone. I'm not angry; I'm not bitter; I'm not offended; I am going to believe the best.* Don't waste your life being angry; instead, be difficult to offend and quick to forgive.

Power Thought: When I pray, I do so without any anger or bitterness in my heart.

God's Love

But God shows and clearly proves His [own] love for us by the fact that while we were still sinners, Christ (the Messiah, the Anointed One) died for us.   ROMANS 5:8

We are loved, accepted, and made right with God because we place our faith in Jesus Christ and the work He accomplished for us on the cross. He paid for our sins and mistakes. He absolved us from guilt and reconciled us with God. So when we stand before God, we have "rightness," not "wrongness." And we have it because He gave it as a gift, not because we earned it.

Once you believe God's love is based on Who He is and what Jesus has done and not on what you do, the struggle is over. You can cancel your "performance" and serve God, not to "get" Him to love you, but because you know that He does love you.

Power Thought: God has proved His love for me through the atoning sacrifice of His Son.

It Only Takes a Spark

It only takes a spark, remember, to set off a forest fire. A careless or wrongly placed word out of your mouth can do that. By our speech we can ruin the world, turn harmony to chaos, throw mud on a reputation, send the whole world up in smoke and go up in smoke with it, smoke right from the pit of hell.

JAMES 3:5–6 THE MESSAGE

As children of God, we can use our mouths and the power of our words to heal relationships or destroy them. The Scripture above shows how major problems are birthed by something as simple as wrong words—a tiny spark can cause an entire forest to catch fire, just as a single word can hurt many people.

Once we have said something, we cannot take it back, so we must be very careful about what we say. If you have said unkind things, apologize, seek forgiveness, and begin to use right words in your life and your relationships.

Power Thought: I am very careful about what I say because my words have power.

All Things Work Together for Good

We are assured and know that [God being a partner in their labor] all things work together and are [fitting into a plan] for good to and for those who love God and are called according to [His] design and purpose.   ROMANS 8:28

Romans 8:28 tells us all things work together for good. It doesn't say all things *are* good, but it does say that all things *work together* for good.

You can be the kind of person who plans things, but who remains calm even if that plan doesn't work out because something unexpected or upsetting happens. Even people who are really positive don't get everything worked out the way they want all the time. But positive people decide to enjoy themselves no matter what happens, and they trust that God will work all things out for good.

———————

Power Thought: I believe God works all things together for good.

Think on These Things

For the rest, brethren, whatever is true, whatever is worthy of reverence and is honorable and seemly, whatever is just, whatever is pure, whatever is lovely and lovable, whatever is kind and winsome and gracious, if there is any virtue and excellence, if there is anything worthy of praise, think on and weigh and take account of these things [fix your minds on them]. PHILIPPIANS 4:8

We can never become excellent in our actions if we don't first make a commitment to become excellent in our thoughts. The Bible teaches us to think on things that are filled with virtue and excellence, things such as believing the best at all times, things that are honorable, just, pure, lovely, and lovable.

What kind of thoughts do you entertain? When you recognize that your thoughts are not good, do you take action to cast them out of your mind or do you lazily let them remain? It is impossible to become an excellent person without first developing an excellent mind. God has called each of us to be excellent in all that we do and to enjoy an excellent life, so if you haven't done it yet, start today thinking in that direction.

Power Thought: My thoughts are full of all that is pure and lovely and worthy of praise.

Hold Your Position

O our God, will You not exercise judgment upon them? For
we have no might to stand against this great company that is
coming against us. We do not know what to do, but our eyes are
upon You.   2 CHRONICLES 20:12

The people in this verse had come to realize three things for certain:
(1) They had no might against their enemies; (2) they did not know
what to do; and (3) they needed to have their eyes focused on God.

Once they came to these realizations and freely acknowledged
them to Him, the Lord said to them: "Be not afraid or dismayed at
this great multitude; for the battle is not yours, but God's.... You
shall not need to fight in this battle; take your positions, stand
still, and see the deliverance of the Lord" (2 Chronicles 20:15, 17).

Your position should be one of waiting on the Lord, with your
eyes focused on Him, worshipping and giving thanks, while He
works all things out for your good.

Power Thought: I keep my eyes on the Lord; the battle
belongs to Him.

Be Positive

What has happened to all your joy?   GALATIANS 4:15 NIV

Many years ago, I was extremely negative. My thoughts were all negative, so my mouth was negative; therefore, so was my life. When I really began to study the Word and to trust God to restore me, one of the first things I realized was that the negativity had to go.

Negative minds produce negative lives, but positive minds produce positive lives. Negative thoughts are full of fear and doubt, but positive thoughts are full of faith and hope.

If you don't have any idea what God's will is for you at this point, you can begin by thinking, *Well, I don't know God's plan, but I know He loves me. Whatever He does will be good, and I'll be blessed.* Begin to think positively about your life; practice being positive in every situation that arises.

Power Thought: I maintain a positive attitude in all circumstances.

The God Habit

And He came out and went, as was His habit, to the Mount of Olives, and the disciples also followed Him.   LUKE 22:39

Jesus didn't frequently go to the Mount of Olives because He liked mountain climbing. He went there to pray. Notice that it was His *habit* to go there, His automatic response not only in times of tribulation, but at *all times*, to spend time with His heavenly Father.

You will find throughout Scripture that all of the great men and women of God had similar habits. They all knew the vital importance of spending time with God.

The Bible says Enoch *habitually* walked with God: "And Enoch walked [in habitual fellowship] with God; and he was not, for God took him [home with Him]" (Genesis 5:24). Hebrews 11:5 explains that Enoch "skipped death completely" (*The Message*). Instead of letting Enoch die, God transferred him directly to heaven because God was pleased with him. Here is a man who developed such an intimate relationship with God that the world could no longer hold him. Enoch developed a "God habit." Seeking and spending time with God is your most vital need.

Power Thought: I have a "God habit"; I habitually walk with God, seeking His face and spending time with Him daily.

Meditate on the Works of God

*Therefore is my spirit overwhelmed and faints within me
[wrapped in gloom]; my heart within my bosom grows numb.
I remember the days of old; I meditate on all Your doings; I
ponder the work of Your hands.* PSALM 143:4–5

The psalmist David talked frequently about meditating on all the
wonderful works of the Lord—the mighty acts of God. He said he
thought on the name of the Lord, the mercy of God, the love of
God, and many other such things.

When he was feeling depressed, he wrote in Psalm 143:4–5
that his response was not to meditate on the problem. Instead,
he actively came against the problem by *choosing* to remember the
good times of past days—pondering the doings of God and the
works of His hands. In other words, David focused his thoughts
on something good, and it helped him overcome depression.

Never forget this: Your mind plays an important role in your
victory. Think thoughts that will add power to your life, not ones
that drain your strength and energy.

Power Thought: I don't waste my time thinking about
things that steal my energy.

Hearing from God

But the Lord was not in the wind; and after the wind an
earthquake, but the Lord was not in the earthquake; and after
the earthquake a fire, but the Lord was not in the fire; and after
the fire [a sound of gentle stillness and] a still, small voice.

1 KINGS 19:11–12

God speaks in a still, small voice. If you want to hear from Him,
create a quiet, peaceful, strife-free atmosphere, and set apart regu-
lar time to fellowship with Him there. He may not always speak
what you want to hear, or in the way you might think that He
would, but don't get discouraged—God will lead you. He rarely
lets us in on His entire plan at the beginning. Obey what you
sense in your heart that you are to do, and when He is ready He
will show you the next thing. And always remember to be thankful. As you do, you will find your sensitivity to God's voice increasing. *He will speak* to you, and *you can hear* from Him. Just get quiet
and listen, and expect Him to lead you in all that you do.

———————————

Power Thought: I can hear the still, small voice of God.

Who You Should Talk To

*Blessed (happy, fortunate, prosperous, and enviable) is the
man who walks and lives not in the counsel of the ungodly
[following their advice, their plans and purposes].*

PSALM 1:1

The Word of God clearly teaches us not to seek or follow the advice
of the ungodly. If you do need advice, get it from a true friend
who will love you enough to disagree with you if necessary. Seek
out someone with mature spiritual character who is making good
decisions about his or her own life before asking that person what
you should do with yours. Also, be sure that person can be trusted
with your secrets if what you are sharing is something private.

If a person tells you someone else's secrets, you can be assured
they will also tell yours; therefore, choose your friends wisely.

Power Thought: I seek wise, godly counsel.

What Is Your Reputation?

[Jesus] stripped Himself [of all privileges and rightful dignity],
so as to assume the guise of a servant (slave), in that He became
like men and was born a human being.

PHILIPPIANS 2:7

You have an inner life and an outer life. Your outer life is your reputation with people. Your inner life is your reputation with God.
The Bible says Jesus "made himself of no reputation" (Philippians
2:7 KJV) because the inner life is what is important to God.

The apostle Paul said, "Now am I trying to win the favor of
men, or of God? Do I seek to please men? If I were still seeking
popularity with men, I should not be a bond servant of Christ (the
Messiah)" (Galatians 1:10). In other words, trying to please people
gives them control and can cause you to lose the call that God has
on your life. Focus on your relationship with God rather than your
reputation with people.

Power Thought: My relationship and reputation with
God are more important than my reputation with people.

New Level, New Devil

There is a wide-open door for a great work here, although many oppose me.　　　　1 CORINTHIANS 16:9 NLT

The Bible tells us that with every opportunity, opposition always comes. The devil always resists our progress. The devil is always ready to prevent the birth of any good thing God tries to do in us or through us. The Bible says, "And the dragon stationed himself in front of the woman who was about to be delivered, so that he might devour her child as soon as she brought it forth" (Revelation 12:4).

To me, this represents the enemy stationed and ready to devour the birth of our successes in every area of life. Every time God puts a fresh, new idea in your heart or gives you a dream, a vision, or a new challenge for your life and you desire to give birth to it, the enemy will be there to oppose you. However, if you know this ahead of time, you can press through the opposition and see God's good will come to pass in your life.

Power Thought: I will not let the devil stand in the way of accomplishing the work God has set before me.

As a Man Thinks...

For as he thinks in his heart, so is he.   PROVERBS 23:7

Our thoughts are very powerful. I believe and say, "Where the mind goes, the man follows." If we think of something unjust that someone has done to us over and over, it will be difficult, if not impossible, to treat that person with God's kindness the next time we see them. Another example is that if we think about food, we usually end up eating it.

Think about what you want to do, not what you don't want to do, because your thoughts will become your actions. Think about forgiving people who hurt you, and you will be able to forgive. Think about being a blessing to others, and you won't end up being selfish. Yes, our thoughts are powerful—and with God's help, we can think on things that will benefit us rather than hurt us.

Power Thought: God helps me think on things that are lovely and pure.

Come Boldly

So let us come boldly to the throne of our gracious God. There we will receive his mercy, and we will find grace to help us when we need it most.   HEBREWS 4:16 NLT

A person who knows who they are in Christ and believes in the power the Bible says they can have will exude an attitude of confidence. When you develop a healthy consciousness of the power you have in Christ, you can approach God's throne *boldly*. You should be spiritually *daring* in your prayers, *confidently* praying for things you know you don't deserve, and stepping out in faith, believing in God's mercy and goodness, believing He will bless you because *He* is good, not because you are.

When you come to know who you are in Christ, you become a person of faith and power who not only confidently enjoys life every day, but who is a wonderful witness to others of the power and goodness of God.

Power Thought: I have the right to come boldly to the throne, with confidence, expecting my prayers to be answered.

Joy in Suffering

Consider it wholly joyful, my brethren, whenever you are
enveloped in or encounter trials of any sort or fall into various
temptations.   JAMES 1:2

A spiritually mature person has a different view of trials and tribulations than an immature person. A spiritually mature person
handles tribulations by keeping joy and trusting God in the midst
of it. Even though the enemy may be bringing it, God is able to
work good out of it, and very often we learn things about ourselves
during trials that we would never see any other way.

We should thank God in the midst of our trials instead of mur-
muring and complaining and feeling sorry for ourselves. Look at
your troubles in a new way. Don't act any differently when you are
going through a storm than you would if life were full of rainbows
(you don't get rainbows until you've been through a storm!). And
remember, with every temptation, He also provides a way out (see
1 Corinthians 10:13).

———————

Power Thought: I have joy even in the midst of my trials.

Trust in Him

Do all things without grumbling and faultfinding and
complaining [against God] and questioning and doubting
[among yourselves].   PHILIPPIANS 2:14

The Scripture above tells us not to complain against God. Since
God is our Father, our Provider, and the One Who watches over
us, when we complain about anything we are basically saying we
don't like what God is doing, and we don't trust His leadership in
our lives. Even if what is happening in our circumstances is not
something God is doing, it is something He can fix if we will trust
Him to do so.

We can judge by our words if we are thankful and appreciative
of God's goodness or if we are discontent. If we truly trust God,
then we won't murmur and complain, but instead we will voice
our thankfulness to Him for working in our lives and giving us the
strength to do whatever we need to do while we are waiting.

Power Thought: I trust God; therefore, I have nothing to
grumble about!

Develop Your Potential

*He Who began a good work in you will continue until the day
of Jesus Christ [right up to the time of His return], developing
[that good work] and perfecting and bringing it to full
completion in you.*   PHILIPPIANS 1:6

Before the days of digital cameras, cameras had film that had to be
taken to a processor or a darkroom for development. Just having
the undeveloped film didn't do you any good. But once you went
through the process of development, you had beautiful pictures
for yourself and others to see.

It's the same with you. God placed potential inside you, but
just having potential is not enough. Be willing to let God work
daily to bring you to spiritual maturity in Him.

It takes time and a willingness to let God work in your life to
develop your potential, but I guarantee you can make a difference
in the world and enjoy an amazing life as you learn to be led by the
Holy Spirit rather than by your own will and ways.

Power Thought: God is at work in my life, developing
and perfecting the potential He placed inside me when He
created me.

A Two-Edged Sword

For the word of God is living and powerful, and sharper than any two-edged sword, piercing even to the division of soul and spirit, and of joints and marrow, and is a discerner of the thoughts and intents of the heart.   HEBREWS 4:12 NKJV

Second Corinthians 10:4–5 teaches us that casting down imaginations, thoughts, reasoning, and theories not in agreement with God's Word requires us to use our *spiritual* weapons, not physical. When we speak the Word of God out of our mouths, it becomes a two-edged sword—defeating the enemy with one edge and opening the blessings of heaven with the other. There are many other *defensive* weapons protecting us from attack, but the Word is *offensive*—it defeats the enemy.

Like any other principle in God's Word, this will not work if it is not applied. Just knowing this information doesn't change anything. Faith needs to be active. It must be released. We can release God's Word through prayer, confessing His Word out loud, and taking God-inspired action.

Power Thought: I am armed for battle with a two-edged sword—the Word of God.

Love People in Your Thoughts

By this shall all [men] know that you are My disciples, if you love one another [if you keep on showing love among yourselves].
JOHN 13:35

One of the most valuable and beautiful things you can do is love others. We can purpose to think about the good things we find in all the people we know, and as we do, our attitudes toward them will improve.

Often we think about what is wrong with people and what we don't like about them. Focusing on people's faults is not showing love to them. We can choose to pray for them concerning any weaknesses they may have, and at the same time pray for ourselves that God will help us in our weaknesses also.

Focus on positive, loving thoughts about people. Then when they do something you don't like, you are already so full of good thoughts about them, it is easy to just let it go.

Power Thought: With my thoughts, I love people and purposely do good to them.

Taming the Tongue

I said, I will take heed and guard my ways, that I may sin not with my tongue; I will muzzle my mouth as with a bridle while the wicked are before me.   PSALM 39:1

The psalmist David prayed a lot about his words. He said, "Let the words of my mouth and the meditation of my heart be acceptable in Your sight, O Lord, my [firm, impenetrable] Rock and my Redeemer" (Psalm 19:14). "Set a guard, O Lord, before my mouth; keep watch at the door of my lips" (Psalm 141:3). We can see from these Scriptures that David was determined not to sin with his tongue, but at the same time, he relied on God for strength to follow through.

One of the things we should ask God each day is to help us speak right things. Our words are very important, and they should be used for God's purpose. We should desire to be mouthpieces for God, speaking His Word faithfully.

Power Thought: With God's strength, I can tame my tongue.

More Than Enough

And my God will liberally supply (fill to the full) your every need according to His riches in glory in Christ Jesus.

PHILIPPIANS 4:19

Paul tells us God will "liberally supply" all of our needs. He doesn't promise God will give us everything we *want*, but he does assure us God will meet our every *need*.

Many times we think of needs in terms of the basic necessities of life. These represent our physical needs, but I believe God created us to need more than these essentials. We don't simply need money, nourishment, a roof over our heads, and clothes to wear. We also need wisdom, strength, health, friends, and loved ones; and we need the gifts and talents and abilities to help us do what we are supposed to do in life. We need many things, and God is willing to meet all of our needs when we trust and obey Him.

Power Thought: God liberally supplies all of my needs.

Who He Is

*I assure you, most solemnly I tell you, he who believes in Me
[who adheres to, trusts in, relies on, and has faith in Me] has
(now possesses) eternal life.*   JOHN 6:47

As long as miracles happen, everybody is willing to follow Jesus.
In John chapter 6, the people followed Jesus because of what He
was doing for them, but Jesus spoke to them about seeking Him
for Who He is and not merely what He does. God wants us to seek
His face, not His hand.

We will have seasons when it seems as if God is silent and still,
almost as though He is hiding from us. He doesn't want us to stop
following Him during those times, but we will if we are seeking
only His hand (what He can do for us). During those seasons,
when God is "hiding" and we are seeking, our faith can grow. If
we are happy only when some big, exciting thing is going on in
our lives, we will never be stable because that's not our routine,
everyday experience. Our normal, natural, everyday lives can be
supernatural when we trust God.

Power Thought: I seek God's face and not His hand. I
want Him, not just what He can do for me.

The Danger of Anger

And become useful and helpful and kind to one another,
tenderhearted (compassionate, understanding, loving-hearted),
forgiving one another [readily and freely], as God in Christ
forgave you.   EPHESIANS 4:32

The word *anger* is one letter removed from the word *danger*.
God's Word tells us not to let the sun go down on our anger (see
Ephesians 4:26). When we stay angry, we give the devil a foothold
in our lives; we open a door for him to work.

God promises His children a blessed and abundant life *if* they
obey His commandments. Staying angry and harboring unkind
feelings toward others is disobedience. God commands us to forgive as freely as He has forgiven us. In this life, we must be very
generous with forgiveness. It is one thing we can learn to give
away every day. If you are angry with anyone for any reason, even
if your anger seems justified, choose to forgive, and you will be
doing yourself a favor.

Power Thought: I am generous with forgiveness.

Are You Trusting or Worrying?

Lean on, trust in, and be confident in the Lord with all your heart and mind and do not rely on your own insight or understanding.

PROVERBS 3:5

Many times we say we are trusting God, but our minds are worrying. As the above verse confirms, we are to trust the Lord not only with our hearts, *but also with our minds.*

What do you allow your mind to do when you have problems? Do you worry and try to figure things out, or do you leave them in God's capable hands? If you operate in the mind of the Spirit, trusting God instead of worrying, you can have "the peace of God, which surpasses all understanding" (Philippians 4:7 NKJV); you can have unspeakable joy (see 1 Peter 1:8) right in the middle of terrible trials and tribulations. Trusting God instead of worrying releases joy in us and provides answers to our problems.

Power Thought: I trust in and lean on my God with all my heart and mind.

Destroy the Strongholds in Your Mind

For the weapons of our warfare are not physical [weapons of flesh and blood], but they are mighty before God for the overthrow and destruction of strongholds.

2 CORINTHIANS 10:4

A stronghold is usually a fortress of negative thoughts the devil establishes in your mind. A stronghold isn't built overnight; it has likely been developing for most of your life, and so it will have to be taken down brick by brick by brick.

Examine yourself and learn what provokes you to think the thought you want to be free from. Does stress or some other negative emotion cause you to turn to negative thoughts? Boredom? Loneliness? Being tired? Sometimes understanding why or when we do something is the doorway to freedom from that thing. Then, with God's help, you can overcome those strongholds. The Word of God becomes your weapon to do battle with when you read it, speak it, pray it, believe it, and sing it.

Power Thought: With God's help, I can tear down the strongholds Satan has set up in my mind.

Find Contentment in God

I know what it is to be in need, and I know what it is to have plenty. I have learned the secret of being content in any and every situation, whether well fed or hungry, whether living in plenty or in want.   PHILIPPIANS 4:12 NIV

When Paul said he had learned to be content, he was saying he still trusted God even if he did not particularly like the situation in which he found himself. Therefore, his trust kept him in perfect peace. When our minds are fixed on the Lord, we are content and peaceful.

Trusting God and refusing to complain in hard times greatly honors Him. There is no value in saying how much we trust God when all is well if, when the test comes, we can't say and sincerely mean, "I trust You, Lord." Through gratitude and thanksgiving, you can close the destructive doors of discontentment. Don't wait until everything is perfect before you decide to enjoy your everyday life.

Power Thought: I am content in all circumstances because my trust is in God.

No Offense

Great peace have they who love Your law; nothing shall offend
them or make them stumble.   PSALM 119:165

There is no doubt about it—as long as we are in the world and
around people, we will have opportunities to be offended. The
temptation to become hurt, angry, or offended comes just as surely
as any other temptation comes, but Jesus said we should pray that
we will not give in to temptation (see Matthew 26:41).

People who want to live powerful lives must become experts at
forgiving those who offend and hurt them. When someone hurts
your feelings or is rude and insensitive, quickly say, "I will not
be offended." If the person is in your presence, you can say these
words quietly in your heart, but later when the memory of what
he or she did returns to haunt you, repeat aloud, "I will not be
offended," and ask God to help you forgive them.

There will be times when God leads you to confront others who
have committed offenses. He may lead you to initiate a necessary
reconciliation. But we should never let the offenses of others cause
us to stumble, to become hard-hearted, or to harbor unforgiveness
in our hearts.

Power Thought: By God's grace, I am difficult to offend.

We Don't Have to Pay for Our Mistakes

My little children, I write you these things so that you may not violate God's law and sin. But if anyone should sin, we have an Advocate (One Who will intercede for us) with the Father—[it is] Jesus Christ [the all] righteous [upright, just, Who conforms to the Father's will in every purpose, thought, and action].

1 JOHN 2:1

Obviously our goal should be to not sin. But if we do sin, God has already provided Jesus—Who is perfect—to take our place and atone for our sin. We may feel we are earning God's forgiveness by feeling guilty. But that is our fleshly way of trying to "pay" for our mistakes. Jesus did not die for us so we could feel guilty; He died for us so we could have an intimate relationship with God through Him. He died so our sins could be forgiven and we could have right standing with God. He wants us to come boldly to the throne of grace in prayer and have our needs met.

Power Thought: Jesus died for my sins so I don't have to pay for them.

Are You at Rest?

*For only we who believe can enter his rest. As for the others,
God said, "In my anger I took an oath: 'They will never enter
my place of rest,'" even though this rest has been ready since he
made the world.*   HEBREWS 4:3 NLT

When you feel frustrated or upset, or if you have lost your peace
and your joy, ask yourself, *Am I believing God's Word?* The only way
to be free from struggling is to believe the Word and obey whatever Jesus puts in your heart to do. Believing God's Word delivers
you from struggling so you can rest in the promises of God.

If your thoughts have become negative and you are full of
doubt, it is because you have stopped believing God's Word and
trusting Him. As soon as you start believing God's Word, your joy
will return and you will be at ease again.

Power Thought: I believe God and His Word, and by
trusting Him, I enter His rest.

Give Yourself to What You Are Doing

Keep your foot [give your mind to what you are doing].

ECCLESIASTES 5:1

When the term *multitasking* first became popular, everyone seemed to want to do it. After this, many job descriptions suddenly included phrases such as "must be able to multitask," and many still do. While there are certainly times a person must juggle responsibilities and handle more than one thing at a time, I am not sure multitasking serves us well in everyday life, and I don't think it should become the normal way to live. In fact, I think trying to do too many things at once creates stress and prevents us from enjoying life.

I challenge you to stop trying to multitask excessively and learn to give yourself to the one thing you are doing at that moment. This kind of concentration requires discipline, but it's worth it because being able to focus helps you enjoy the present moment.

Power Thought: I live in the present moment and focus my full attention on the task at hand.

Focus

Therefore, holy brothers and sisters, who share in the heavenly calling, fix your thoughts on Jesus, whom we acknowledge as our apostle and high priest.   HEBREWS 3:1 NIV

Focusing on good things makes us feel good, excited, energized, and enthusiastic. When we focus our time and attention on things we find to be bad, we feel sad, angry, or anxious. That's why it's so important for us to "fix our thoughts on Jesus" and keep our focus on Him. God has given us the ability to choose happiness no matter what is going on around us. I am not suggesting we ignore our problems, but there is a big difference between focusing on them—worrying about them—and working to solve or resolve them.

A negative person cannot be happy, and a persistently positive person cannot be unhappy, at least not for any lengthy period of time. Choose to have a happy life by focusing on Jesus. Do what you can do to take care of any responsibility you have with your problem, and while you are waiting for God to do what you cannot do, you are free to go ahead and enjoy your life.

Power Thought: My mind is focused only on Jesus and good things.

An Attitude of Expectancy

"For I know the plans I have for you," says the LORD. *"They are plans for good and not for disaster, to give you a future and a hope."*   JEREMIAH 29:11 NLT

Live with an attitude of expectancy. King David said, "Yet I am confident I will see the LORD's goodness" (Psalm 27:13 NLT). He expected and was confident in his expectation.

To live expectantly is not the same as living with a sense of entitlement, which is an attitude that says we *deserve* everything. We don't deserve anything from God, but because of His great love and His mercy for us, He wants us to live in holy expectancy so we can receive His best.

Even if you have been needy all your life, that can change if you will do your part. Your part is to obey God, sow good seeds, have a vision of abundance, and think and say right things in agreement with God's Word—and be persistent. As you continue doing this, you will develop a healthy mind-set enabling you to prosper in all areas.

Power Thought: I expect good things to happen in my life today.

Learning to Wait Well

But let endurance and steadfastness and patience have full play and do a thorough work, so that you may be [people] perfectly and fully developed [with no defects], lacking in nothing.

JAMES 1:4

Patience is extremely important for people who want to glorify God and enjoy their lives. If one is impatient, the situations they encounter in life will certainly cause them to react emotionally in a wrong way. The next time you have to wait on something or someone, instead of just reacting, try talking to yourself a little. You might think, *Getting upset will not make this go any faster, so I might as well enjoy the wait.* Then perhaps say out loud, "I am developing patience as I wait, so I am thankful for this situation." When you do this, you are acting on the Word of God rather than reacting to the unpleasant circumstance.

Power Thought: While I wait, I develop more patience, so I am going to enjoy the wait.

"But God"

And the patriarchs [Jacob's sons], boiling with envy and hatred
and anger, sold Joseph into slavery in Egypt; but God was with
him.   ACTS 7:9, emphasis added

God doesn't want us to ignore or deny our circumstances, but He
does want us to deny their right to control us through negative
thinking. Joseph was a young boy sold into slavery by his very own
brothers, "but God was with him," and eventually Joseph became
second in command over all of Egypt. I believe that even though
Joseph had difficult circumstances, he knew God was greater than
them.

Learn to think and say, "I may have problems, but God is with
me." One might think, *I lost my job*, but God *is faithful.* Another
may think, *My husband left me with our two kids*, but God *is our*
Provider. I had to think, *I was abused*, but God *has promised me*
double for my trouble. I didn't get to go to college, but God *promoted*
me anyway. The sick person can think, *I have health problems*, but
God *is my healer.*

No matter what you don't have, you do have God—and with
Him, all things are possible.

Power Thought: I may not like all my circumstances, *but*
God is with me and He will cause me to succeed.

Change and Transition

Readily adjust yourself to [people, things] and give yourselves to humble tasks. Never overestimate yourself or be wise in your own conceits.   ROMANS 12:16

Everything changes except God, and letting all the changes in our lives upset us won't keep them from happening. People change, circumstances change, our bodies change, and our desires and passions change. There is one certainty in life: change!

Our thoughts are the first things we need to deal with during change because thoughts directly affect our emotions and determine our behavior. When circumstances change, make the transition mentally and your emotions will be a lot easier to manage. If something changes that you are not ready for and did not choose, you will more than likely have a variety of emotions about the change, but by acting on God's Word and not merely *re*acting to the situation, you will be able to manage your emotions instead of allowing them to manage you.

———————————

Power Thought: I don't resist and dread change, and I adapt when I need to.

Be a God-Pleaser

Now, am I trying to win the favor of men, or of God? Do I seek to please men? If I were still seeking popularity with men, I should not be a bond servant of Christ (the Messiah).

GALATIANS 1:10

The Bible says Jesus "made himself of no reputation" (Philippians 2:7 KJV). That is a significant statement. He was not well thought of by many people, but His heavenly Father approved of Him and what He was doing, which was all that really mattered to Him. As long as you and I have God's approval, we have what we need most.

The apostle Paul said if he had been trying to be popular with people, he would not have been a servant of the Lord Jesus Christ. Paul was saying that if we have an unbalanced need for the approval of people, it will hinder the fulfillment of our destiny. We cannot always be God-pleasers and people-pleasers at the same time. Strive to please God, and let Him deal with people.

———————————

Power Thought: I put God first in my life and want to please Him.

God Loves You!

Even as [in His love] He chose us [actually picked us out for Himself as His own] in Christ before the foundation of the world, that we should be holy (consecrated and set apart for Him) and blameless in His sight, even above reproach, before Him in love. EPHESIANS 1:4

God tells us in His Word how much He loves us and accepts us, and even though He already knew every mistake we would ever make, He actually chose us for Himself. We read it, but we have a difficult time receiving it.

After all, how could God, Who is perfect, be pleased with us in our imperfections? He can because He separates who we are from what we do. As believers in Jesus Christ, we are God's children. We may not always act the way He wants us to, but we never stop being His children and He never stops loving us.

Power Thought: God chose me because He loves me!

Live to Please the Spirit

*Those who live only to satisfy their own sinful nature will
harvest decay and death from that sinful nature. But those who
live to please the Spirit will harvest everlasting life from the
Spirit.*   GALATIANS 6:8 NLT

When we live to please the Spirit, we should expect good results.
If we respect our physical bodies—eat nutritious food and drink
ample water, get plenty of sleep and eliminate excessive stress—
we can expect a harvest of good health. If we are friendly, we will
have friends. If we are generous, we will experience generosity
returned. This is true in every area of our lives, including health,
finances, abilities, relationships, and everything else pertaining to
our well-being. This is one of the most simple laws to understand
and one that produces great power in our lives.

———————————

Power Thought: I live to please the Spirit and expect
good results.

Evidence of Deliverance

*And do not [for a moment] be frightened or intimidated in
anything by your opponents and adversaries, for such [constancy
and fearlessness] will be a clear sign (proof and seal) to them of
[their impending] destruction, but [a sure token and evidence] of
your deliverance and salvation, and that from God.*

PHILIPPIANS 1:28

The apostle Paul said in Philippians we should not, even for one
moment, be frightened or intimidated by anything our opponents
try to do to us. He said our fearlessness is a sign to our enemies of
their impending destruction and evidence of our deliverance and
salvation through God. In other words, when we have trials, the
spiritual world is watching. God is watching and Satan is watching; therefore, how we respond and what we say and do are very
important. If you can hold your tongue and remain emotionally
stable during times of difficulty, then you are honoring God and
letting the devil know he is not going to control you.

Power Thought: I am fearless in all circumstances,
trusting God for my deliverance.

A New Day

Therefore if any person is [ingrafted] in Christ (the Messiah) he is a new creation (a new creature altogether); the old [previous moral and spiritual condition] has passed away. Behold, the fresh and new has come!   2 CORINTHIANS 5:17

As "a new creation," you don't have to allow the old things that happened to you keep affecting you. You're a new person with a new life in Christ. You can have your mind renewed by studying God's Word and learning about His good plan for you. Good things are going to happen to you, and you can start believing that.

It is unwise to refuse to face reality; however, if our reality is negative, we can still have a positive attitude toward it. Always be ready mentally to face whatever comes, believing God works good out of all things.

Rejoice! It's a new day!

Power Thought: I am a new creation in Christ.

Receive His Grace

According to the grace (the special endowment for my task) of
God bestowed on me, like a skillful architect and master builder
I laid [the] foundation, and now another [man] is building
upon it.   1 CORINTHIANS 3:10

Grace is the power of the Holy Spirit coming to us freely, enabling
us to do with ease what we could never do on our own. You might
find other definitions describing grace as God's divine favor, and
that is certainly true, but His grace is also the power you need to
live in victory. Grace can be received only through faith, and that
is one of the main reasons we must resist fear. When we allow fear
to rule us, we unwittingly receive what Satan has planned for our
lives. But when we live by faith through grace, God is able to work
His divine plan in us. Whatever you need to do today, lean on God
and let Him empower you to be successful.

Power Thought: By God's grace I have the skills to do all
He asks of me with ease.

To Love God, Love People

If anyone says, I love God, and hates (detests, abominates) his brother [in Christ], he is a liar; for he who does not love his brother, whom he has seen, cannot love God, Whom he has not seen.   1 JOHN 4:20

Love is much more than a good feeling about someone. Love is a decision. When we are instructed in God's Word to "put on love" (see Colossians 3:14), it means we are to *choose* to love people. It is something we do *on purpose*, whether we feel like it or not. Love is displayed in how we treat people, not how we feel about them.

Part of walking in love is freely forgiving people. A refusal to forgive our enemies drives a wedge between us and God. The Bible actually states that you cannot say you love God if you don't love your brother and sister in Christ. If you want God's will in your life, then do things His way—love and forgive others.

Power Thought: To express my love for God, I show God's love to people.

A Solid Foundation

So everyone who hears these words of Mine and acts upon them [obeying them] will be like a sensible (prudent, practical, wise) man who built his house upon the rock.

MATTHEW 7:24

A solid foundation is the most important part of a building. Without a solid foundation, the building won't last long. Everything else concerning the building is built on the foundation. If the foundation is weak or cracked, nothing built on it is safe. It could crumble or fall apart at any time, especially if stress is placed on it by a storm.

The Bible encourages people to build their lives on the solid rock of Christ, rooted securely in Him (see Matthew 7:24–27 and Ephesians 3:17). If you try to build your life on what people say and think of you, how they treat you, how you feel, or your past mistakes, you are building on sinking sand. But if you trade that old, cracked foundation for a solid foundation, one based on Christ and His love, nothing can shake you.

Power Thought: Christ is my foundation.

Think What God Thinks

Then the way you live will always honor and please the Lord,
and your lives will produce every kind of good fruit. All the
while, you will grow as you learn to know God better and
better.   COLOSSIANS 1:10 NLT

Do you want to be emotionally stable and consistently content? Meditate on God's Word and make sure your thoughts are in line with it. Stop concentrating on wrong things, and start thinking, *No matter what is going on in my circumstances, I am able to remain calm and loving while I trust God to take care of everything.*

Come into agreement with God and His Word. Think what He thinks and say what He says. Will you ever falter in your commitment to think and say positive things? Yes, you probably will, but Colossians 1:10 says we will steadily grow as we learn and do God's will. Just remember, when you fall, all you have to do is get up and try again.

Power Thought: My life is pleasing to the Lord; I am learning to think as God thinks.

Share His Nature

And because of his glory and excellence, he has given us great and precious promises. These are the promises that enable you to share his divine nature and escape the world's corruption caused by human desires.   2 PETER 1:4 NLT

The devil tries to tell us we can't be like God—we *can't* be merciful and gracious; we *can't* have joy; we *can't* be slow to anger and quick to forgive. But the Bible says God has shared His divine nature with us; it is in us, thus we can develop it and it can come out of us.

Don't listen to the devil's lies. Believe instead the promises of God: you *can* be like God in your nature; you *can* have unspeakable joy; you *can* be merciful, never again holding a grudge. Fill your thoughts and words with God's promises. Apply the truth of His Word to your daily life, and you will finish your course with joy (see Acts 20:24)!

Power Thought: I don't have to live as the world lives; I can live as God would because His divine nature is in me.

Believe and Confess

For with the heart a person believes (adheres to, trusts in, and relies on Christ) and so is justified (declared righteous, acceptable to God), and with the mouth he confesses (declares openly and speaks out freely his faith) and confirms [his] salvation.   ROMANS 10:10

We see a pattern in the book of Romans, which teaches us that in order to be saved, we must *believe* in our hearts and *confess* with our mouths. Another version of the Scripture above says simply:

"If you confess with your mouth that Jesus is Lord and believe in your heart that God raised him from the dead, you will be saved. For it is by believing in your heart that you are made right with God, and it is by confessing with your mouth that you are saved" (Romans 10:9–10 NLT).

So I say we should believe and speak, speak and believe—the two work together for our salvation, as well as in every other area of our lives. If we need to believe and speak to receive the salvation that Jesus has provided, then we should live according to the same principle to receive all of God's promises.

Power Thought: Jesus is Lord, and I speak my faith confidently and freely.

He Renews My Strength

But they that wait upon the LORD shall renew their strength;
they shall mount up with wings as eagles; they shall run, and
not be weary; and they shall walk, and not faint.

ISAIAH 40:31 KJV

When you think of an eagle soaring, you probably envision a lone bird flying majestically against a bright blue sky. This is because eagles soar alone. Something about the character, the strength, and the nature of the eagle gives it the courage to soar by itself.

If you want to be an "eagle Christian," you may have to make decisions that separate you from the pack, enabling you to reach altitudes higher than the people around you want to go. Being an eagle means you want to please God more than you want to please people and that you will make your decisions accordingly.

Spending time with God, allowing Him to renew your strength, will help with many things, even things like not losing your temper or saying words you later regret. Make a decision today to rise above mediocrity and soar with the eagles.

Power Thought: When I am weary, I run to God, and He renews my strength.

Be a Blessing

It is more blessed (makes one happier and more to be envied) to give than to receive.

ACTS 20:35

For many years, I could quote the verse above, but I obviously didn't really believe it because I spent my time trying to *be* blessed rather than to be a blessing. But I learned we do not even know what "happy" is until we forget about ourselves, start focusing on others, and become generous givers in every way.

Many people learn about giving in church, and that's good practice for the way we are to live our everyday lives. Don't merely give offerings; be a giver. Every day, pray for God to show you how you can give of yourself and be a blessing to others. As you become a generous giver, you will be amazed at how happy you will be and how much you will enjoy life. Why? Because givers are simply happy people, and it truly is more blessed to give than to receive.

Power Thought: I am a giver, I love people, and I enjoy helping them.

Be Excited

Never lag in zeal and in earnest endeavor; be aglow and burning with the Spirit, serving the Lord.

ROMANS 12:11

Excitement, zeal, and passion are positive emotions. They energize us to press forward in our pursuits. The Bible instructs us to be zealous and enthusiastic as we serve the Lord. God instructs us to be enthusiastic and burning with zeal even when He chastises or corrects us (see Revelation 3:19). Why should we do that? Simply because He expects us to trust that everything He does is for our ultimate good.

Good emotions come from good decisions and good thoughts. Don't get up each day and wait to see how you feel, letting those feelings dictate the course of your day. Instead, set your mind in the right direction ahead of time and make decisions you know will produce emotions you can enjoy.

Power Thought: I serve the Lord with energy and excitement.

Live in the Present

So do not worry or be anxious about tomorrow, for tomorrow will have worries and anxieties of its own. Sufficient for each day is its own trouble.   MATTHEW 6:34

There is a reason God called Himself "I AM" (see Exodus 3:14). Not "I was" or "I will be," but "I AM." The greatest gift anybody has is the present moment.

Be determined to give yourself and your mind completely to what you are doing (see Ecclesiastes 5:1). No matter where your body is, you are where your mind is. If your mind is somewhere else, you can't enjoy where you are. For example, if you're in church, but your mind is on your grocery list, then you aren't getting anything spiritually from the sermon being preached.

Start doing everything you do unto the Lord—to Him, for Him, with Him—and you will be able to focus on each moment of the present and enjoy life.

———————

Power Thought: I live in the present and enjoy each moment of the day.

Love Your Life

I came that they may have and enjoy life, and have it in abundance (to the full, till it overflows).

JOHN 10:10

The more we speak about something, the more of that something we have. For example, if you talk about all the things you don't like, you will dislike them even more, but talking about love will increase the ability to love in your life.

Very few people learn this blessed lesson: Love the life you have and never compare yourself, or what you have, to anyone else. Learn to love everything except evil. If you dislike something, change it if you can. If you don't like your job, look for a different one. If you don't like your neighborhood, move. If you don't like the weather, realize you can't change it and change your attitude. As Reinhold Niebuhr said: "God, grant me the serenity to accept the things I cannot change, courage to change the things I can, and wisdom to know the difference."

The more you are filled with loving thoughts and the more you speak loving words, the happier you will be.

Power Thought: I love everything and everyone in my life, even my enemies.

Go the Extra Mile

Let your light so shine before men that they may see your moral excellence and your praiseworthy, noble, and good deeds and recognize and honor and praise and glorify your Father Who is in heaven.   MATTHEW 5:16

It is very easy to be a mediocre person. All you have to do is make no extra effort of any kind and compromise all of your beliefs. If you compromise, it means you do a little less than you know is right and proper; but to be excellent means to do a little more than you might have to in order to get by—it means going the extra mile.

Peace is one of the greatest rewards you receive when you make an effort to do things the way you know they should be done. Choose the more excellent way, and then you will find that God's peace is yours.

Power Thought: I always strive for excellence and go the extra mile.

God Is with You

The LORD himself goes before you and will be with you; he will never leave you nor forsake you. Do not be afraid; do not be discouraged.   DEUTERONOMY 31:8 NIV

God has promised He will never leave you nor forsake you. No matter what you are going through in life, you do not have to go through it alone. Every day with God is not going to be a perfect day with no problems. But your worst day with Jesus will still be better than your best day without Him.

Say all throughout the day, "God is with me right now. Right now, God is with me. God is with me when I go to work. God is with me when I go to the marketplace. God is with me. He's not just with me when I go to church; God is with me all the time. He cares about everything I do."

Power Thought: God is with me at all times; I never have to walk alone.

Start Strong, Finish Well

*Therefore, since we are surrounded by such a great cloud of
witnesses, let us throw off everything that hinders and the sin
that so easily entangles, and let us run with perseverance the
race marked out for us.*   HEBREWS 12:1 NIV

Typically, we are excited at the beginning of an opportunity, a relationship, or a venture; we're also happy when we can celebrate
our achievements and have the satisfaction of fulfilled desires. But
between the beginning and the end, every situation or pursuit has
a "middle"—and the middle is where we often face our greatest
challenges, hurdles, roadblocks, obstacles, detours, and tests.

The enemy wants you to stop short of receiving and enjoying
everything God has for you, and he will tempt you to give up by
sometimes making the middle of your venture seem too long or
too hard. God, on the other hand, wants the very best for you; He
wants you to finish the race set before you, enjoying every step
along the way. Be determined to be faithful all the way through
and enjoy your victory.

Power Thought: I will not give up. I will run my race with
perseverance and finish with joy.

What Must I Do to Please God?

But without faith it is impossible to please and be satisfactory to Him.   HEBREWS 11:6

In John 6:28–29, some people asked Jesus what He required of them: "What are we to do, that we may [habitually] be working the works of God? [What are we to do to carry out what God requires?] Jesus replied, This is the work (service) that God asks of you: that you believe in the One Whom He has sent."

Hebrews 11:6 tells us that it is impossible to please God without faith in His Son. God's love for us is unconditional, and it's important for us to understand that He wants us to do good works because of our love for Him and our faith in Jesus—not because we feel we have to earn His love. It blesses God when we live by faith, working through His love in our hearts (see Galatians 5:6).

Power Thought: As I put my faith in Christ, I can know with confidence that I am pleasing to Him.

Christ's Sufficiency

I have strength for all things in Christ Who empowers me [I am ready for anything and equal to anything through Him Who infuses inner strength into me; I am self-sufficient in Christ's sufficiency].   PHILIPPIANS 4:13

Most people have experienced some kind of circumstance that truly seemed impossible to them. But the fact of the matter is you *can* do whatever you need to do in life.

As a believer in Jesus Christ, you are full of the Spirit of God, and nothing is too difficult for you if God is leading you to do it. God will not call you to do anything that He will not enable and empower you to do. He will not allow you to go through anything impossible.

God guarantees us the strength for everything we need to do because He Himself empowers us; we are sufficient (which is another way of saying we have everything we need) because of His sufficiency. You can do whatever you need to do today and every day!

Power Thought: I am self-sufficient because I have Christ's sufficiency.

When to Say No

Jesus said to them, My food (nourishment) is to do the will (pleasure) of Him Who sent Me and to accomplish and completely finish His work.   JOHN 4:34

It seems that a fear of saying no to people is one of the reasons why we make commitments we don't keep.

Many people don't have the courage to say no. They don't want to hurt people or make them angry so either they say yes, not intending to follow through, or they say they will do something and then make excuses based on untruths to avoid doing it. Everyone who makes a request wants to hear yes, but wouldn't you rather someone be unhappy because you said no than to have them unhappy because you said yes and didn't keep your word?

You should follow the leading of the Holy Spirit and say yes only when you are led to. You are responsible to be obedient only to God, not to keep everyone in the world happy by doing everything they want you to do.

———————

Power Thought: I am committed to do only the work God has called me to do.

Remind God of His Promises

I have set watchmen upon your walls, O Jerusalem, who will never hold their peace day or night; you who [are His servants and by your prayers] put the Lord in remembrance [of His promises], keep not silence.

ISAIAH 62:6, emphasis added

Imagine a child coming to his father and saying, "Dad, you promised you would play ball with me tonight." That is a beautiful example of a child who is confident in his dad's love. But it can be a bit more difficult to believe we can go to Father God in the same way, reminding Him of His promises to us.

According to the Word, however, you have *the right*, through Christ, to go boldly to the throne in Jesus' name with your requests. You see, God actually *wants* you to remind Him in your prayers of His promises as you wait for Him to fulfill His plan for your life.

Power Thought: I will remind the Lord of His promises to me.

Forgiving Those Who Hurt Us

*So be merciful (sympathetic, tender, responsive, and
compassionate) even as your Father is [all these].*

LUKE 6:36

One of the reasons it can be difficult to forgive others when we
are offended is that we have told ourselves probably thousands of
times forgiving is hard to do. We have convinced ourselves and set
our mind to fail at one of God's most important commands, which
is to forgive and pray for our enemies and those who hurt and
abuse us (see Luke 6:35–36).

While praying for our enemies and blessing those who curse us
may seem extremely difficult or nearly impossible, we can do it if
we believe that we can. Having the proper mind-set is vital if we
want to obey God. Everything He tells us to do is for our benefit,
and He will always give us the ability to do what He asks us to do.

Power Thought: I show compassion and forgiveness to all
people.

The Characteristics of a Mature Christian

When I was a child, I talked like a child, I thought like a child, I reasoned like a child; now that I have become a man, I am done with childish ways and have put them aside.

1 CORINTHIANS 13:11

The mature believer is a person who learns to do the will of God no matter how it feels or how difficult it is. A mature believer works with the Holy Spirit continuously to be changed into the image of Jesus Christ—learning to say what God says and live a life dedicated to God and His purposes.

God's goals for you are to mature spiritually and no longer be controlled by your own thoughts, emotions, and desires. He wants you to learn His Word and direct your life accordingly, being ready at all times to be His representative in the Earth.

Power Thought: I have put aside childish ways and now talk, think, and reason like a mature Christian.

How to Increase Your Faith

So let us seize and hold fast and retain without wavering the hope we cherish and confess and our acknowledgement of it, for He Who promised is reliable (sure) and faithful to His word.

HEBREWS 10:23

Giving voice to your faith can actually increase your faith—because what you say out loud gets rooted in your heart. I have heard that we believe more of what we say than what anyone else says, so why not say things that we truly want to believe? Say frequently, "I trust God," or "I believe God is working in my life and circumstances right now." Say, "God loves me and will work through me to do good to other people."

The Psalms are filled with confessions of faith: "I will say of the Lord, He is my Refuge and my Fortress, my God; on Him I lean and rely, and in Him I [confidently] trust!" (Psalm 91:2). You can make a similar confession!

The apostle Peter said we should resist the devil at his onset (see 1 Peter 5:9). Developing the habit of confessing your faith as soon as any negative thoughts, words, behaviors, and attitudes appear will increase your faith and your joy. Soon you'll be living from faith to faith (see Romans 1:17), without wavering.

Power Thought: God is faithful; my hope in Him is unwavering.

Real Love

*I give you a new commandment: that you should love one
another. Just as I have loved you, so you too should love one
another.* JOHN 13:34

Some people think of love as a sensation—a wonderful feeling of
excitement or gushy emotions that make us feel warm and cozy all
over. While love certainly has its wonderful feelings and powerful
emotions, it's so much more than that.

Real love is a decision concerning the way we behave in our
relationships with other people. Real love meets needs even when
sacrifice is required in order to do so. The Bible makes this point
in 1 John 3:18: "Let us not love [merely] in theory or in speech but
in deed and in truth (in practice and in sincerity)." Clearly, love
moves us to take action—not just to theorize or talk. If we want
to be like Jesus, we need to love others with the same kind of gracious, forgiving, generous, unconditional love He extends to us.

Power Thought: God loves me, and I love all people.

Be Led by the Spirit

Now the Lord is the Spirit, and where the Spirit of the Lord is, there is liberty (emancipation from bondage, freedom).

2 CORINTHIANS 3:17

One of the most dynamic ways to keep your joy is to allow the Holy Spirit to lead you (see Psalm 139:24). If you pray first, asking God for a plan, He will never push you into a work of the flesh. Instead, His Holy Spirit prompts, guides, and gently leads you to a place of joy; He will never manipulate or control you. If you are too consumed with your own plan, too locked into the way you think things ought to be, you won't even hear God speak to you or recognize the promptings from Him. If you are too determined to follow your own ritualistic rules, you can miss the gentle leading of the Holy Spirit and lose the joy God intends for you to have.

It is not wrong to have a plan, but always offer your plan to God and tell Him that if He has something else in mind, you are willing to submit to Him.

Power Thought: The Spirit of the Lord has led me out of bondage and into a life of freedom and joy.

Respond as God Would

Do all things without grumbling and faultfinding and complaining [against God] and questioning and doubting [among yourselves]. PHILIPPIANS 2:14

I know people who have been sick or have had other difficult problems for an extended period of time and yet have the most beautiful attitudes. They never complain, are not grouchy, don't act as if the world owes them something, and don't blame God or even feel sorry for themselves. But I also know people with the same sorts of circumstances who talk only about their illnesses and problems and how hard it all is for them. They are self-absorbed and often easily offended, bitter, and resentful.

Every situation in life requires making a decision about how you are going to respond. If you respond the way God would, then your trials are much easier to handle. I highly respect and admire people who are able to be stable even when they are in tremendous pain and discomfort. I think they are a wonderful example to all of us.

Power Thought: I am very careful about what I say at all times.

Bless Those Who Curse You

Invoke blessings upon and pray for the happiness of those who curse you, implore God's blessing (favor) upon those who abuse you [who revile, reproach, disparage, and high-handedly misuse you].   LUKE 6:28

To *bless* means "to speak well of." When someone has hurt you, you can refuse to speak evil about them, even if you're tempted to do so. You can also bless them by talking about their good qualities and the good things they have done.

Speaking well of someone who has hurt you is probably the last thing you feel like doing, but doing it puts you in the "God league." It puts you on the road less traveled, the one Jesus Himself traveled on. Don't forget, one of the last things He did was forgive someone who didn't deserve forgiveness, and He did it while hanging on a cross being crucified. Forgiving our enemies and refusing to speak evil of them shows our willingness to obey God, and it releases blessings in our lives.

Power Thought: I speak well of my enemies and pray for God to bless them.

With All Your Heart

*You shall love the Lord your God with all your heart and with
all your soul and with all your mind (intellect). This is the great
(most important, principal) and first commandment.*

MATTHEW 22:37–38

When the Pharisees asked Jesus what the most important commandment of all was, He responded: Love the Lord with all your
heart.

You can't simply love God when you need Him to help you; you
can't love Him only when it's convenient or popular; you shouldn't
pay attention to Him just when you're at church or because you
think He might punish you if you don't. No! You are to love Him
because He is wonderful and amazing—not out of fear or obligation. And you are to love Him *passionately.* That's what "with all
your heart" means.

God is good, and He deserves our love! Determine to seek and
love God with all your heart from this moment on.

Power Thought: I love God with all that I am.

Learning to Adapt and Adjust

*Live in harmony with one another; do not be haughty
(snobbish, high-minded, exclusive), but readily adjust yourself
to [people, things] and give yourselves to humble tasks.*

ROMANS 12:16

If we don't learn to adapt and adjust to people and things, we will
break under the strain of life. This requires humility, trust in God,
and a strong commitment to being a maker and maintainer of
peace.

A man who lived to be 114 years old gave this tip about lon-
gevity: "Embrace change, even when it slaps you in the face." We
don't invite all the changes in life that come our way, but if we
can't make them go away, we can embrace them.

When you have a circumstance that wasn't part of your plan or
that you didn't invite into your life, ask yourself if you can change
it. If you can't, then embrace it, let God help you deal with it, learn
from it, and move on.

Power Thought: God has given me the ability to adjust to
people and things and remain in peace.

Believe

May the God of your hope so fill you with all joy and peace
in believing [through the experience of your faith] that by the
power of the Holy Spirit you may abound and be overflowing
(bubbling over) with hope.   ROMANS 15:13

According to the Scripture above, how can I be filled with joy
and peace? *By believing.* Not by doubting or being negative, but
by believing. We all believe something, but believing only God's
Word produces the results mentioned in the Scripture for the day.
By just being positive, having the best perspective on everything,
and always believing the best of everybody, we release peace and
joy in our lives. We get what we believe, what we think, and what
we meditate on, so believe God's Word and expect peace and joy.

Power Thought: I believe God's Word in every situation
in my life, and I have peace and joy.

A Balanced Attitude

However, we possess this precious treasure [the divine Light of
the Gospel] in [frail, human] vessels of earth, that the grandeur
and exceeding greatness of the power may be shown to be from
God and not from ourselves.   2 CORINTHIANS 4:7

Pride is very dangerous. Many great men and women of God have
fallen into sin due to pride. Don't fall into the trap of pride, but
don't go to the other extreme and think self-rejection, self-hatred,
and self-abasement are the answer. Instead, seek to be what I call
an "everything-nothing" person—everything in Christ and nothing without Him.

Jesus Himself said that apart from Him, we can do nothing (see
John 15:5). Be confident, but remember, the strength resulting
from confidence can quickly be lost in conceit. It is vital to remain
humble. God deserves all the credit and glory for any good work
manifesting in our lives.

Power Thought: The exceeding greatness in me is Jesus.

A Cure for the Insecure

If you set your heart aright and stretch out your hands to
[God] ... then can you lift up your face to Him without stain [of
sin, and unashamed]; yes, you shall be steadfast and secure;
you shall not fear.   JOB 11:13, 15

In Ephesians 3:17 the apostle Paul writes: "May Christ through your faith [actually] dwell (settle down, abide, make His permanent home) in your hearts! May you be rooted deep in love and founded securely on love." The Greek word for *secure* means "without anxiety." If you are a Christian, through Jesus, you have a right to enjoy a life without anxiety. It also means to "have full command." You can resist insecurity and not be defeated by it as you trust and rely on Jesus.

True security doesn't depend on how much money you have, your job, the way you look, how others respond to you, or even how they treat you. Security is not based on your education, your marital status, the label inside your clothing, the car you drive, or what kind of house you live in. True security is found in trusting Christ alone and knowing that you are loved and taken care of by Him.

Power Thought: My security comes from who I am in Christ.

Control Your Mouth, Enjoy Your Life

For the Scriptures say, "If you want to enjoy life and see many happy days, keep your tongue from speaking evil and your lips from telling lies."   1 PETER 3:10 NLT

The Bible says that we need to control our tongues if we want to enjoy life, and I believe we all want to enjoy life. I find that reading and meditating on what God's Word says about the power of words is helpful to me. Here are some of my favorites:

"Those who control their tongue will have a long life; opening your mouth can ruin everything" (Proverbs 13:3 NLT).

"Let the words of my mouth and the meditation of my heart be acceptable in Your sight, O Lord, my [firm, impenetrable] Rock and my Redeemer" (Psalm 19:14).

"If anyone considers himself religious and yet does not keep a tight rein on his tongue, he deceives himself and his religion is worthless" (James 1:26 NIV).

Look up these additional Scriptures and meditate on them as you seek to live a powerful life: Proverbs 8:8; 11:9; 12:18; 15:4; 18:21. God's Word has power in it that will strengthen and enable you to speak words of life that will benefit you.

Power Thought: I am careful and intentional about all that I say.

Prevent Disappointment

They trusted in, leaned on, and confidently relied on You, and were not ashamed or confounded or disappointed.

PSALM 22:5

There is nothing unusual or wrong about initial feelings of disappointment, but it is what we do from that point forward that makes all the difference in the world. Absolutely nobody gets everything they want all the time, so we need to learn how to deal properly with disappointment.

Trusting God completely and believing that His plan is infinitely better for you than your own will prevent you from being disappointed with God. You might feel anger toward your situation, but don't ever be angry with God. When you get angry, you naturally want to lash out at someone, but it is unwise to make God your target. He is the only One Who can help you and truly comfort you; therefore, it is much better to run *to Him* in your time of pain than away from Him.

_____

Power Thought: I trust God completely and am never disappointed with Him.

God Cares How You Treat People

If I had the gift of prophecy, and if I understood all of God's
secret plans and possessed all knowledge, and if I had such faith
that I could move mountains, but didn't love others, I would be
nothing.   1 CORINTHIANS 13:2 NLT

I truly believe that how we treat the people in our lives is very
important to God. He loves people and wants us to love people as
part of our service to Him.

People may forget what you said and what you did, but they will
never forget how you made them feel. Make each individual feel
as if they matter and are valuable. Speak encouraging words, give
gifts, and spend quality time with others. Listen with interest to
what people say; make a big deal out of anything good that anyone does and shrug off their mistakes because we all make them.
Be gentle, patient, and loving to each person you meet. There are
many ways you can be good to other people, but they all boil down
to love.

Power Thought: I treat everyone with love.

A Holy Reminder

But the Helper, the Holy Spirit, whom the Father will send
in My name, He will teach you all things, and bring to your
remembrance all things that I said to you.

JOHN 14:26 NKJV

The Holy Spirit can remind you of—"bring to your remembrance"—a Scripture when you need it, *if* you have the Word of God in you.

For example, if you believe the devil's lie that you have to earn God's love, you are going to be extremely frustrated trying to do something you can't do. But if you have taken the time to learn the Word, meditate on the Word, and speak the Word, the Holy Spirit will bring to mind any number of Scriptures about God's free and unconditional love when you need them. He will remind you of God's life-giving principles and energize you to follow them.

Study the Word so the Holy Spirit has a deep reservoir of Scripture to pull from when you need Him to "bring to your remembrance" all that He has said.

Power Thought: The Word lives inside me, and the Holy Spirit reminds me of the Scriptures I need at just the right time.

Focus on the Positive

Fix your thoughts on what is true, and honorable, and right,
and pure, and lovely, and admirable. Think about things that
are excellent and worthy of praise.

PHILIPPIANS 4:8 NLT

Robert Schuller said, "The good news is that the bad news can be turned into good news when you change your attitude." And if you can't muster up a good attitude concerning something you're unhappy about, you can at least try to downplay the negative.

If you will make a decision to say as little as possible about your problems and disappointments in life, they won't dominate your thoughts or your mood. Talk as much as possible about your blessings and hopeful expectations, and it will increase your joy. Be sure each day is filled with words that fuel joy, not anger, depression, bitterness, or fear. Talk yourself into a better mood! Find something positive to say in every situation.

Power Thought: My thoughts and words are focused on positive and hopeful things.

Worry Is No Good

And who of you by worrying and being anxious can add one unit of measure (cubit) to his stature or to the span of his life?
MATTHEW 6:27

Worrying does us absolutely no good. It doesn't change anything, and we waste time by being upset over things we can't do anything about. The Bible says we can't even add one inch to our height by worrying. Yet we often worry, worry, worry, which gets us nowhere.

Every time we get upset, it takes a lot of emotional energy, tires us out, can harm our health, steals our joy, and still doesn't change one thing. We need to stop trying to fix things only God can fix.

Jesus essentially tells us to calm down (see John 14:27) and cheer up (see John 16:33). I believe these two things combined serve as a one-two knockout punch to the devil. When you realize you can't fix everything, you calm down; and when you know God can, you cheer up!

Power Thought: I refuse to worry; worrying doesn't change a thing.

Four Steps to Victory in Forgiveness

*And let us not be weary in well doing: for in due season we shall
reap, if we faint not.*   GALATIANS 6:9 KJV

You cannot make wrong feelings go away any more than you can
make right ones come, but God can and will. If you will simply
do what Scripture instructs you to do, you will be able to work
through the process of forgiveness.

The first thing you decide is to forgive those who have hurt
you; the second thing is to pray for them. Another thing God tells
you to do is to bless your enemies. To bless someone means to
speak well of them and want good things for them. Refuse to talk
unkindly about those who hurt you. Don't keep talking about
what your enemies did; it only keeps the pain stirred up in you.
The fourth thing you must do is wait. Don't give up. Keep doing
what is right, and wait on God to change your feelings and He will.

Power Thought: Forgiveness is a process; God gives me
the strength to walk it out.

Talk to Yourself

Be filled with the Spirit; speaking to yourselves in psalms and hymns and spiritual songs.   EPHESIANS 5:18–19 KJV

One way you can get over being controlled by your emotions is by talking to yourself. You can talk yourself into emotions, such as anger and jealousy, and you can also talk yourself out of them.

For example, you can talk yourself *into* being angry when somebody mistreats you by focusing on the offense, thinking about it, and telling others about what happened. But you can also talk yourself *out* of being angry—just get away from what is making you mad for a few minutes and start talking to yourself in a different way: *Okay, self, just settle down. Don't give the devil an open door. Don't get mad, losing your temper and saying a lot of things you are going to be sorry for later.*

Remember, Satan is the enemy—the source of your anger—not man (see Ephesians 6:12).

Power Thought: By talking to myself in a calm and positive way, I can overcome anger.

From Glory to Glory

*And all of us, as with unveiled face, [because we] continued
to behold [in the Word of God] as in a mirror the glory of the
Lord, are constantly being transfigured into His very own
image in ever increasing splendor and from one degree of glory
to another; [for this comes] from the Lord [Who is] the Spirit.*
2 CORINTHIANS 3:18

When you receive Christ as your Savior, you receive the ability to
do everything God wants you to do. God would never expect you
to be patient if He didn't give you patience. He would never expect
you to love if He didn't put love in you to give away.

But all of this comes in seed form, and seeds must be watered
to grow. The Bible says we are to water them with the Word. God
changes you from glory to glory as you stay in His Word and are
transformed into His image. Receive God's Word as one of the
most precious gifts that God offers, and watch it change you. You
are even changing right now as you read this devotional!

Power Thought: As I study the Word of God diligently, I
am transformed into His image.

Seeking God

But without faith it is impossible to please and be satisfactory to Him. For whoever would come near to God must [necessarily] believe that God exists and that He is the rewarder of those who earnestly and diligently seek Him [out].   HEBREWS 11:6

Seeking God is central to our walk with Him; it is vital for spiritual progress. But what exactly does it mean to seek God?

One way we seek God is to think about Him—thinking about His Word, His ways, what He has done for us, how good He is, and how much we love Him. Thinking about His goodness will cause us to desire a better relationship with Him simply because of Who He is, not because of what He can do for us. As you seek Him regularly, you will come to know Him more intimately and realize that He is your loving Father, Who cares about every aspect of your life.

Power Thought: I seek God at all times, and I love to spend time with Him.

Freedom from Anxiety

Do not fret or have any anxiety about anything, but in every circumstance and in everything, by prayer and petition (definite requests), with thanksgiving, continue to make your wants known to God.   PHILIPPIANS 4:6

I highly recommend speaking the Word of God when a "worry attack" comes upon you. Doing this is what it means to wield the two-edged sword against the enemy (see Hebrews 4:12 and Ephesians 6:17). A sword in its sheath won't do any good during an attack; God has given us the sword of His Word so we can use it! Learn Scriptures like Philippians 4:6, and when the enemy attacks, counter his attack with the same weapon that Jesus used: the Word.

The Word coming from a believer's mouth, with faith to back it up, is the single most effective weapon that can be used to win the war against worry and anxiety.

_____

Power Thought: I am free from worry and anxiety.

God Is Just

Instead of your [former] shame you shall have a twofold recompense; instead of dishonor and reproach [your people] shall rejoice in their portion. Therefore in their land they shall possess double [what they had forfeited]; everlasting joy shall be theirs.   ISAIAH 61:7

Justice is one of God's amazing and admirable character traits. He brings justice as we wait on Him and trust Him to be our Vindicator when we have been hurt or offended. He simply asks us to pray and forgive—and He does the rest. He makes even our pain work out for our good (see Romans 8:28). He justifies, vindicates, and recompenses us. He pays us back for our pain if we follow His commands to forgive our enemies, and He even gives us double for our trouble. Refuse to live in unforgiveness, and trust God to reward you for any mistreatment you have endured.

Power Thought: God gives me double for my trouble.

I Obey God Promptly

But if one loves God truly [with affectionate reverence, prompt obedience, and grateful recognition of His blessing], he is known by God [recognized as worthy of His intimacy and love, and he is owned by Him].   1 CORINTHIANS 8:3

The more we love God, and the more we receive His love, then the more we are able to obey Him promptly and reverently. We should realize that all of God's commands are things that will benefit our lives. When God tells us not to do something, He is never trying to take something away from us. Instead, He is protecting us from something harmful. Loving God means that we trust Him, and when we do trust Him, we are able to trust His direction in our lives. If you are having difficulty doing something that you know God wants you to do, or not doing something you know He doesn't want you to do, remember that He loves you and is trying to help you—trust Him and obey.

Power Thought: I love and trust God, and I obey Him promptly.

Humility Is Loving Others

Let each of you esteem and look upon and be concerned for not [merely] his own interests, but also each for the interests of others.　　　　PHILIPPIANS 2:4

Humble people are quick to repent when they do something wrong. Humble people always apologize if they have hurt or offended somebody. They are willing to listen to reason and seriously consider the opinions of others. Truly humble people are not rude because they value other people. They realize other people are equally as valuable as they are. Truly humble people give credit to God and others who help them get where they are. Humble people show appreciation, taking the time to thank others.

Jesus teaches us that truly great people serve others. Humility is needed in order to serve others with a right motive and good attitude. Beware of pride, and always pray that God will keep you humble.

Power Thought: I appreciate people and care about their needs.

Thoughts and Words

From a wise mind comes wise speech; the words of the wise are persuasive. Kind words are like honey—sweet to the soul and healthy for the body.   PROVERBS 16:23–24 NLT

These verses show us that our thoughts and words are intimately connected—our words come from our thoughts. They are like joints and marrow, so close it is hard to divide them (see Hebrews 4:12). Because of this, we must have pleasant thoughts so we can also have pleasant words.

It is not possible to think bad thoughts and then speak good words, for out of the heart, the mouth speaks (see Matthew 12:34). Many people think they cannot control their thoughts, but that is not true. We can choose what we want to think about and should do so carefully because our thoughts become our words and our words affect our lives in many ways.

When a thought comes into your mind that you know will not bear good fruit or is not pleasing to God, cast it out. Refuse to take it and meditate on it, but rather replace it with something that will produce joy and peace in your life.

Power Thought: My thoughts and words are intimately connected. To speak godly words, I will think positive thoughts.

With Thanksgiving

Enter into His gates with thanksgiving and a thank offering and into His courts with praise! Be thankful and say so to Him, bless and affectionately praise His name!   PSALM 100:4

God's Word teaches us not to worry, but to come to Him, in every circumstance, *with thanksgiving* (see Philippians 4:6). Psalm 100:4 says we cannot even come into the presence of God unless we come with thanksgiving.

If we want assurance of answered prayer, we should pray with thanksgiving, not with complaining. People who complain are showing, by their attitude and words, that they do not trust God and are not thankful or appreciative. You may be a person who genuinely loves God, but you may also have a habit of complaining and have not, until now, realized how disrespectful it is to God. If you are convicted of sin in this area, there is no condemnation, but you should ask God to forgive you and begin to fill your prayers with praise and thanksgiving.

Power Thought: My prayers are filled with gratitude and thanksgiving.

A Great Big Happy Life

Therefore do not be vague and thoughtless and foolish, but understanding and firmly grasping what the will of the Lord is.
EPHESIANS 5:17

It's God's will for us to grow up and mature spiritually. It's God's will for us to have good relationships. It's God's will for us to have good lives.

If you've had a negative past, it's because the enemy interfered and got in. No matter what you went through or what you might be going through right now, you can be positive about your future. Think about it positively; talk about it positively.

It's a bad attitude to say, "I guess I'll just have more of what I've always had." I encourage you to have a positive vision for your future. God says people without vision perish (see Proverbs 29:18). No matter what has happened in the past, no matter what is going on right now, you can believe something great will happen in your future.

Power Thought: Something good is going to happen to me today.

Learn to Enjoy Yourself

And I will say to my soul, Soul, you have many good things laid up, [enough] for many years. Take your ease; eat, drink, and enjoy yourself merrily.   LUKE 12:19

A root cause of a lot of our unhappiness is simply that we are not happy with ourselves. We may not be happy with the way we look, our talents, or our imperfections. We may compare ourselves with others instead of happily being the people we are intended to be.

We all make mistakes, and although we want to be serious about the changes that need to be made in our lives, it is also good to learn to laugh at ourselves and not be so intense about every little mistake we make. The best thing you can do is lighten up and don't take yourself so seriously!

You are with "you" more than you are with anyone else, so if you can learn to enjoy your own company, it will greatly improve the quality of your life. Learn to enjoy yourself!

Power Thought: I enjoy my own company; I enjoy being with myself!

Believe the Best

Love bears up under anything and everything that comes, is ever ready to believe the best of every person, its hopes are fadeless under all circumstances, and it endures everything [without weakening].   1 CORINTHIANS 13:7

Believing the best about people is very helpful in the process of forgiving people who hurt or offend us. As human beings, we tend to be suspicious of others, and we often get hurt due to our own imaginations. It is possible to believe others hurt you on purpose when, in reality, they are not aware they did anything at all and would be grieved to know they hurt you. God calls us to love others, and love always believes the best.

I encourage you to believe the best about others. Resist the temptation to question their motives or to think they hurt you intentionally. Believing the best about others will keep offense and bitterness out of your life and help you to stay peaceful and joyful. So always do your best to believe the best.

Power Thought: I believe the best about every person.

Your Attitude Speaks for You

A good person produces good things from the treasury of a good heart, and an evil person produces evil things from the treasury of an evil heart.   MATTHEW 12:35 NLT

You don't always have to verbalize your thoughts for people to see them. Think about how you act on a first date with someone you like. You show signs of acceptance and approval. You smile a lot, and you encourage him or her with your eyes and head nods to show your interest. You haven't said a word, but your body language says: "I like you!" Now think about how you act when you are in the grocery line and the cashier is taking forever. You shift your weight from side to side, cross your arms, huff, or even roll your eyes. Again, your posture speaks for you. You may think your thoughts are hidden, but your thoughts show up in your attitudes, body language, words, and actions. Make sure you display a good attitude.

Power Thought: I will think good, godly thoughts so I can have a good heart and attitude.

Wisdom Encourages Patience

A man's wisdom gives him patience.   PROVERBS 19:11 NIV

People often ask me, "How can I learn contentment and stability?" One way, straight out of the Bible, is patience.

God wants us to use wisdom, and wisdom encourages patience. Wisdom silently tells us to *wait a little while, until the emotions settle down, before you do or say something. Then check to see if you really believe it's the right thing to do.* Emotions urge us toward haste, telling us we must do something and do it right now! But godly wisdom tells us to be patient and wait until we have a clear picture of what we are to do and when we are to do it. I like to say it like this: Let emotions subside and then decide. We need to be able to step back from our situations and see them from God's perspective. Then we need to make decisions based on what we know rather than what we feel.

Power Thought: I have the wisdom to develop patience and emotional stability.

Practice Listening

And your ears will hear a word behind you, saying, This is the way; walk in it, when you turn to the right hand and when you turn to the left.　　　　　ISAIAH 30:21

One of the ministries of the Holy Spirit is to lead us into God's will for each of our lives: "But when He, the Spirit of Truth (the Truth-giving Spirit) comes, He will guide you into all the Truth (the whole, full Truth)" (John 16:13).

People frequently pray for God to tell them what to do in specific situations. And while divine guidance is God's will for all His children, before we can hear from Him, we must *believe* it is our inherited right to do so.

Discerning the voice of God will take some practice—you need to practice listening—and you will probably make a few mistakes. But don't be afraid to step out in faith. Be willing to listen, to learn, and to be led.

Power Thought: The Lord is my Guide, and I hear His voice.

Feeling Fear Is Not Cowardly

For God hath not given us the spirit of fear; but of power, and of love, and of a sound mind.   2 TIMOTHY 1:7 KJV

When the Bible says "God hath not given us the spirit of fear," it does not mean we will never feel fear. Feeling fear is part of being alive. We may feel fearful when we are doing something we have never done before, or when obstacles seem insurmountable. But this does not mean we are cowards; it simply means we are human. It is cowardly only when we allow our fears to dictate our actions or decisions instead of following our hearts.

Feeling fear is not the same as being afraid—which means letting fearful feelings control our actions. I might feel angry, but I can still choose not to act on my anger and instead respond with forgiveness and love. In the same way, we can feel fear while not letting it influence our decisions.

Power Thought: In Christ, I have a spirit of power, love, and a sound mind.

God Loves You Unconditionally

For I am persuaded, that neither death, nor life, nor angels, nor principalities, nor powers, nor things present, nor things to come, nor height, nor depth, nor any other creature, shall be able to separate us from the love of God, which is in Christ Jesus our Lord.   ROMANS 8:38–39 KJV

Love—knowing you're loved—is what every person wants. Every person wants to feel valuable. Every single person wants to feel that he or she matters.

Guess what? God loves you unconditionally. He doesn't love you because of anything you do or don't do; God just loves you. There's nothing you can do about it. You can't buy His love. You can't get rid of His love. Nothing can separate you from the love of God.

You are created by the hand of God, on purpose, and you are an unrepeatable miracle. There is nobody else exactly like you. There never will be anybody else exactly like you. And God has an amazingly wonderful plan for your life.

Power Thought: God loves me unconditionally, and nothing can separate me from His love.

Seek to Do Good

See that none of you repays another with evil for evil, but always aim to show kindness and seek to do good to one another and to everybody.   1 THESSALONIANS 5:15

The very thought of anything good increases my joy. I love to do good things for people, and I enjoy it when people do good things for me.

I want to emphasize the words *aim* and *seek* in the Scripture above, to call attention to the fact that doing good is possible only when we actively seek to do so. Make doing good, being good, and speaking good things your goals in life. If you do, you can expect more joy than you have ever experienced.

Remember: The "Good Book" introduces us to the "Good Shepherd," Who brings "Good News" and introduces us to the "Good Life" He preordained for us to live. He wants us to say good things and be good to everyone! This simple yet profound principle can and will change the world.

Power Thought: I love to do good.

Renew Your Mind

*Put on your new nature, and be renewed as you learn to know
your Creator and become like him.*   COLOSSIANS 3:10 NLT

Many times the problems we experience are because we are reacting to our situations out of the old nature instead of the new nature
that is ours in Christ. Our minds need to be renewed according to
the new lives God has given us. When they are, we begin to look
at situations in a new way, and we begin to react based on God's
truth and His character.

For example, the moment you have a challenge or a problem,
your renewed mind will say: "I don't worry about anything. I put
my trust in God." The moment you start to feel upset about something: "I am content and emotionally stable." The minute someone
aggravates you: "I am adaptable. I am difficult to offend."

The Word of God is a treasure. As we hear it, learn it, receive it,
believe it, and speak it, we are making an investment that will pay
glorious dividends throughout our lives.

Power Thought: God has given me a new nature, and I
am learning to think as He thinks so I can do what He
would do in every situation.

Time with God

*Keep on asking and it will be given you; keep on seeking and
you will find; keep on knocking [reverently] and [the door] will
be opened to you.*   MATTHEW 7:7

We all have the same amount of time each day, but some people
regularly find time to spend with God while others never do. I
have found that when we say we "don't have time to spend with
God," it's simply an excuse.

The truth is, if you spend time with God, He will multiply what
you have left. Like the little boy with the loaves and fish who gave
Jesus his small lunch for use in feeding thousands of people and
ended up with more food left over than he began with (see John
6:1–14), you will end up with more time than you would have had
by leaving God out of your busy schedule.

At this moment, you are as close to God as you want to be.
What you sow, you will reap, so if you want a bigger harvest, then
you simply need to sow more seed. If you want a closer relationship with God, spend more time with Him. He wants you to find
more peace and joy in His presence.

Power Thought: I want to be as close to God as I can get,
so I will spend time with Him every day.

The Glory of God

Jesus said to her, Did I not tell you and promise you that if you would believe and rely on Me, you would see the glory of God?

JOHN 11:40

When Jesus stood in front of the tomb of Lazarus, intending to raise him from death, Martha spoke out of her fear, saying, "But Lord, by this time he [is decaying and] throws off an offensive odor, for he has been dead four days!" (John 11:39).

Jesus responded with, "Did I not tell you and promise you that if you would believe and rely on Me, you would see the glory of God?" (v. 40).

The word *glory* means the "manifestation of God's excellence." Seeing the glory of God does not necessarily mean you get things the way you want them, when you want them, all the time. But it does mean you can trust God for His best in every situation. You can relax and trust God because He will always take care of you.

———————

Power Thought: I believe I will see God's glory.

Believe in Prayer

Don't worry about anything; instead, pray about everything.
Tell God what you need, and thank him for all he has done.

PHILIPPIANS 4:6 NLT

How many problems have you solved by worrying? How much time have you spent worrying about things that didn't end up happening? Has anything ever gotten better as a result of your worrying about it? Of course not!

The instant you begin to worry or feel anxious, give your concern to God in prayer. Release the weight of it and totally trust Him to either show you what to do or take care of it Himself.

Prayer is the blueprint for a successful life. During His time on Earth, Jesus prayed. He entrusted everything to God—even His reputation and life. We can do the same. Don't complicate your communication with God. Believe in Him and ask Him for what you need through simple, confident prayers.

Power Thought: Worry accomplishes nothing. I trust in the Lord.

Change Your Mind, Change Your Life

Study this Book of Instruction continually. Meditate on it day and night so you will be sure to obey everything written in it. Only then will you prosper and succeed in all you do.

JOSHUA 1:8 NLT

When we say "meditate," we generally mean to choose what we want to think about and roll it over and over in our minds until it becomes a part of us.

Take a look at this quote:

"If you continue to believe as you have always believed, you will continue to act as you have always acted. If you continue to act as you have always acted, you will continue to get what you have always gotten. If you want different results in your life, all you have to do is change your mind" (Anonymous).

You will never do what you need to do until you think what you need to think. God's Word will renew your mind, so love the Word, live the Word, speak the Word, meditate on the Word—and things will begin to change.

Power Thought: As I meditate on God's Word, my thoughts will change and then my life will change.

Set Your Mind Ahead of Time

If then you have been raised with Christ [to a new life, thus sharing His resurrection from the dead], aim at and seek the [rich, eternal treasures] that are above, where Christ is, seated at the right hand of God. And set your minds and keep them set on what is above (the higher things), not on the things that are on the earth.   COLOSSIANS 3:1–2

Colossians 3:2 tells us to set our minds and keep them set. To "set your mind" means you make a firm decision about how to handle a situation and you keep your mind set in that direction. It means to be single-minded, not double-minded. We can prepare ourselves to handle a difficult situation properly by setting our minds ahead of time—telling ourselves no matter what comes, we can do it. If you're in a less than desirable situation, but you know it is where God wants you to be, don't drift off into thinking that can weaken you. Instead, think, *I am strong in Christ, and I can do whatever He leads me to do.*

Power Thought: I set my mind and keep it set for victory.

I Wonder . . .

For this reason I am telling you, whatever you ask for in prayer, believe (trust and be confident) that it is granted to you, and you will [get it].   MARK 11:24

In this verse, Jesus did not say, "Whatever you ask for in prayer, *wonder* if you will get it." Instead, He said, "Whatever you ask for in prayer, *believe* that you will receive it—and you will!"

We are much better off thinking something positive than just wondering all the time about everything imaginable. Instead of wondering what kind of grades your son will get on his report card, you can believe that he will make good grades. Rather than wondering what you should wear to the party, you can decide what to wear. Instead of wondering what you should do about a problem you have and how to solve it, you can turn it over to God and think on purpose, *I trust God with this situation, and He will work it out.* Don't waste your time "wondering" when you can believe!

Power Thought: I believe I will receive an answer to my prayers.

Believe You Are Free

*Even so consider yourselves also dead to sin and your relation
to it broken, but alive to God [living in unbroken fellowship
with Him] in Christ Jesus.*   ROMANS 6:11

If you want to stop doing the wrong things and start doing the right
things, you must believe it's possible. If you try to conquer wrong
things while your thoughts and words are filled with doubt and
unbelief, you are not likely to experience the victory you desire.
Even if you have tried a thousand times previously and have never
been successful, believe *this time* will be different.

God's Word says we are dead to sin—our relationship with it
is broken—and we are alive to God, living in unbroken fellowship with Him. Spiritually speaking, that means you are *already
free* from doing wrong, and you just need to believe it and start
applying the freedom Jesus purchased for you with His death and
resurrection.

Power Thought: I am alive to God and dead to sin; I am
free!

Always Be Content

Keep your lives free from the love of money and be content with what you have, because God has said, "Never will I leave you; never will I forsake you."   HEBREWS 13:5 NIV

Finances can play a big part in a person's sense of contentment. We would all like to always have more money than we need; however, for most of us, there are times in life when that is not the case. It is important for us to keep a good attitude either way.

As long as we are breathing on this Earth, we are going to encounter a mixture of things we like and things we don't like, but God wants us to be content with what we have—no matter what. Being content shows that we trust God to provide for us what He knows is right at the time. Dave and I experienced many years of very meager finances, and they were difficult years, but we realize now that we learned a lot during that time and have come to appreciate it. Having a good attitude in lean times will help you get through them faster and with greater joy.

Power Thought: I will always have Jesus; therefore, I can be content no matter what.

Think God Thoughts

Instead, let the Spirit renew your thoughts and attitudes.

EPHESIANS 4:23 NLT

Not every thought in your head is from you, your circumstances, or God. Some of it is from Satan, placing wrong thoughts in your brain because he wants to control your life. Did you know you don't have to continue thinking on everything that comes to your mind? You can cast wrong thoughts down and replace them with right thoughts (see 2 Corinthians 10:5).

You may ask, "Do you mean if I wake up and I feel depressed, I don't have to go around being depressed all day?"

Exactly! When you wake up and think, *This is not going to be a good day*, instead, you can believe, *The devil is a liar. This is the day the Lord has made. I will rejoice and be glad. This will be a fantastic day!*

Negative thoughts and attitudes can be avoided simply by saying, "That's not a God thought. I cast it down in Jesus' name, and I am going to think something beneficial to me today."

Power Thought: I choose to think Spirit-filled, life-giving thoughts.

Able and Stable

For even though I am absent in body, nevertheless I am with you in spirit, rejoicing to see your good discipline and the stability of your faith in Christ.   COLOSSIANS 2:5 NASB

Many people feel able and qualified to do a particular thing, and yet they live frustrated lives because the right doors don't ever seem to open for them to do that particular thing. Their opportunities never come. Why? I believe many people are "able but not stable." God has given people abilities, but they may not have made the effort to mature and develop a stable character.

God must be able to trust us, and other people must be able to depend on us.

When we are stable and mature in character, we can do what is best no matter how we happen to feel. As long as we are breathing, we are going to have times of abundance and times when we struggle, times when circumstances are up and times when they're down. Let circumstances do what they will; meanwhile, be determined to remain stable.

Power Thought: I am able and stable, regardless of my circumstances.

Give Yourself Permission

For we who have believed (adhered to and trusted in and relied on God) do enter that rest.   HEBREWS 4:3

God doesn't want us to be angry with ourselves because we have weaknesses. When we stop worrying and cast our cares upon Him (see 1 Peter 5:7), His strength will begin to flow through us and change us.

God will be perfecting His work in you right up until Christ returns (see Philippians 1:6). If the good work God is doing in you will continue throughout your life here on Earth, then why be frustrated with all the changes that need to be made? Yes, it's important for us to keep moving forward in our relationship with God every day, making progress in becoming more like Him, but we can enjoy ourselves while God is changing us. You can enter His rest concerning what remains to be done in your personality, character, and life. Study God's Word, trust Him, and thank Him daily that He is working in you.

Power Thought: I believe in God; therefore, I can enter His rest.

God Chooses the Weak

[No] for God selected (deliberately chose) what in the world is
foolish to put the wise to shame, and what the world calls weak
to put the strong to shame.   1 CORINTHIANS 1:27

God gives us His power (grace) so we can do what is needed in
spite of our weaknesses. In fact, God purposely chooses the weak
and foolish things of the world to work through so we will give
Him the glory for what is being done. God wants to amaze the
world, and one of the ways He does so is by accomplishing great
things through people who are weak and don't have the natural
ability to complete the task at hand (see 1 Corinthians 1:25–29).

Relax; don't be afraid you won't be able to do what God has
given you to do. Step out in faith, and God will meet you where
you are and give you His grace (undeserved favor and power) to
complete the task. Through Christ you can do all things!

Power Thought: God uses my weaknesses to show His
strength.

Small Beginnings

*Do not despise these small beginnings, for the L*ORD *rejoices to*
see the work begin, to see the plumb line in Zerubbabel's hand.
ZECHARIAH 4:10 NLT

The Bible tells us to not despise the day of "small beginnings." In
other words, don't waste the beginning of your journey by being
discontent or impatient with how far you have yet to go.

Contentment is the ability to enjoy where you are while you are
on the way to the fulfillment of your dreams. Don't wait until you
reach your destination to enjoy life. Life is more about the journey
than the destination, and even when we do reach one destination,
we usually begin a journey toward another. It is a tragedy to never
enjoy our journeys in life. Each phase of the journey has something in it of value, and I encourage you not to miss any of it.

Power Thought: I refuse to let a bad attitude ruin any
part of my journey; I will enjoy where I am while I'm on
the way to where I'm going.

From Love to Self-Control

But the fruit of the Spirit is love, joy, peace, patience, kindness, goodness, faithfulness, gentleness and self-control. Against such things there is no law.

GALATIANS 5:22–23 NIV, emphasis added

Love and self-control are like bookends that hold the rest of the fruit of the Spirit in place. All of the fruit initially grow from love and are kept in place by self-control. Desiring to walk in the fruit of the Spirit is a good thing because it involves being patient, kind, humble, displaying good manners, not being selfish, and other good fruit as well. Although it would be nice if we automatically behaved that way toward people, it rarely happens without self-control.

We may be able to do it sometimes, but then at other times we may not feel well or a day might be frustrating, and walking in the fruit of the Spirit is more difficult. But thank God He has given us self-control to hold the good fruit in place in our lives.

Power Thought: God helps me display self-control in order to show love to people at all times.

God Loves You Even When You Make Mistakes

But God shows and clearly proves His [own] love for us by the fact that while we were still sinners, Christ (the Messiah, the Anointed One) died for us.   ROMANS 5:8

Have you ever wondered if you are good enough for God to love you? Unfortunately, many people believe God loves them only as long as they don't make mistakes.

Perhaps it was this outlook that caused the psalmist to ask, "What is man that You are mindful of him?" (Psalm 8:4). Yet the Bible tells us we are God's creation, the work of His hands, and He loves each one of us unconditionally.

Let's face it: Jesus didn't die for you because you were great and wonderful; He died for you because He loves you. God loves you, and He wants you to believe it and receive His love all the time—even when you make mistakes.

———————

Power Thought: God's love for me is unconditional.

We Eat Our Words

From the fruit of his words a man shall be satisfied with good.
                                                              PROVERBS 12:14

I am sure you have heard someone say, "You are going to eat those words." It may sound like just a phrase to us, but as the Scripture above attests, we do eat our words!

What you say affects not only you, but it affects others as well. The words that come out of your mouth go into your ears as well as other people's, and then they drop down into your soul where they give you either joy or sadness, peace or upset, depending on the types of words you have spoken.

You can also resist wrong thoughts because they are the beginning of wrong words and think on good, healthy ones that produce good things in your life. I always say, "Where the mind goes, the man follows." You could also say, "Where the mind goes, the mouth follows!"

———————————

Power Thought: I am going to eat my words, so I will choose good words that will produce a satisfying life.

Your Everyday, Ordinary Life

So here's what I want you to do, God helping you: Take your everyday, ordinary life—your sleeping, eating, going-to-work, and walking-around life—and place it before God as an offering. Embracing what God does for you is the best thing you can do for him.   ROMANS 12:1 THE MESSAGE

There are dozens of things pertaining to ordinary, everyday life, and you can enjoy them all if you just make a decision to do it. Things like getting dressed, driving to work, going to the grocery store, running errands, keeping things organized, and hundreds of other things. After all, they are the things life is made up of. Begin doing them for the love of God, and realize that through the Holy Spirit you can enjoy absolutely everything you do. Joy doesn't come merely from being entertained, but from a decision to appreciate each moment you are given as a rare and precious gift from God.

Power Thought: I enjoy my life and rejoice in the everyday, ordinary aspects of it.

Persevere in Right Thinking

For the rest, my brethren, delight yourselves in the Lord and continue to rejoice that you are in Him. To keep writing to you [over and over] of the same things is not irksome to me, and it is [a precaution] for your safety.   PHILIPPIANS 3:1

We must consistently choose right thinking, right words, and right action. It's not what you choose to do right one time that's going to change your life. It's doing it over and over and over. I frequently tell people, "When you get so tired of doing it you think you can't stand it, you do it again and again and again and again." Persistence always pays off, and the Bible says that the diligent person will be successful. Don't ever give up!

If you're the kind of person who refuses to give up, I can assure you that you will get your breakthrough and enjoy a lot of victory in your life.

———————

Power Thought: I never get tired of doing what is right.

Make Your Mind Up

Set your minds and keep them set on what is above (the higher things), not on things that are on the earth.   COLOSSIANS 3:2

You may not realize how strong you are when you set your mind on something. This works in both positive and negative ways. If you set your mind on things above, the devil cannot stop you, but if you set your mind on the things of men and have a wrong mind-set, it is difficult to receive God's help. God can show you the truth in His Word, but you won't accept it if you have set your mind against His will and His ways.

If your mind is truly set, nothing will change it. Make your mind up that you are going to live for God's glory and you aren't going to let anything change your mind.

Power Thought: My mind is set on God.

Receive God's Favor

For whoever finds me [Wisdom] finds life and draws forth and
obtains favor from the Lord.   PROVERBS 8:35

Develop your faith in the area of God's favor; live expecting it all
the time. Pray for favor. Trust God to open the right doors and
to close the wrong ones. Ask the Lord for "divine connections"
and friendships that are right for you. Confess that you have favor
with God and He gives you favor with humankind. Before embark-
ing on any business venture, ask for favor. When you meet new
people, ask for favor. I even ask God for favor before going into
a restaurant. He can get me the best seat in the house, the best
waiter, the best service, and the best food.

The Bible says in James 4:2, "You do not have, because you do
not ask." Start asking for favor regularly, and you will be amazed at
the acceptance and blessings coming your way.

Power Thought: I have favor everywhere I go.

Equipped for Hard Things

For this commandment which I command you this day is not
too difficult for you, nor is it far off.   DEUTERONOMY 30:11

"This is too hard" is one of the excuses we hear most frequently.
But we are equipped by God's Spirit to handle hard things. We are
anointed to press through and see victory. The next time you are
tempted to say something is too hard, look at Deuteronomy 30:11,
which says, "It is not too difficult!"

Anything God leads you to do, you can do. God never leads you
to do something unless He gives you the power and the ability to do
it. Prepare yourself for right action with power thoughts. Think, *I
don't know how I'm going to do it, I don't feel like I can do it, but God is
leading me to do it. And I believe if He is leading me to do it, then I can.
Because I believe I can do whatever I need to do through the power of
God that resides in me.*

Power Thought: *Nothing* God asks of me is too difficult.

Make a List

Thank [God] in everything [no matter what the circumstances may be, be thankful and give thanks], for this is the will of God for you [who are] in Christ Jesus [the Revealer and Mediator of that will].   1 THESSALONIANS 5:18

To help you achieve and maintain a new level of contentment in your life, I encourage you to make a list of everything you have to be thankful for. It should be a long list, one that includes little things as well as big things. Why should it be long? Because we all have a lot to be thankful for if we just look for it.

The next time you have lunch or coffee with a friend, resolve to talk about the things you are thankful for. The Bible says we are to be thankful and say so. Meditating on what you have to be thankful for every day and verbalizing it will be amazingly helpful to you.

Power Thought: I am a very thankful person.

Don't Be Double-Minded

[For being as he is] a man of two minds (hesitating, dubious, irresolute), [he is] unstable and unreliable and uncertain about everything [he thinks, feels, decides].   JAMES 1:8

Of course you want to be able to know *for certain* what God wants you to do in every situation, but you don't; and like everyone else, you must step out in faith and eventually do one thing or the other.

Pray with all your heart that if what you are doing is wrong, God will graciously close the door before you make a huge mistake. If you don't have peace about something, then you should not do it. If after prayer and waiting you feel you don't have a clear direction from God, then it may mean He is simply giving you the freedom of making your own choice. If you do make a decision that turns out to be wrong, God will meet you where you are and get you back on the right path. One thing is for sure: God is merciful, and we don't have to be afraid to make decisions. The best way to learn is to begin doing!

Power Thought: I am not afraid to make a decision.

Relax and Trust God Completely

I pray that God, the source of hope, will fill you completely with joy and peace because you trust in him. Then you will overflow with confident hope through the power of the Holy Spirit.

ROMANS 15:13 NLT

If you know you can't fix the problem you have, why not relax while God works on it? It sounds easy, but it took many years for me to be able to do this. I know from experience the ability to relax and accept whatever happens in life is dependent upon our willingness to trust God *completely*.

If things don't go your way, instead of getting upset, start believing that your way was not what you needed and that God has something better in mind for you. God will give you what is best for you, even if it isn't what you think you want! The minute you recognize He is in control, your soul and body relax, and you will be able to enjoy life.

Power Thought: My hope is in God, and I trust Him completely.

A Spiritual Mind

For those who are according to the flesh and are controlled by its unholy desires set their minds on and pursue those things which gratify the flesh, but those who are according to the Spirit and are controlled by the desires of the Spirit set their minds on and seek those things which gratify the [Holy] Spirit.

ROMANS 8:5

If you are walking in the flesh, it's because you put your mind on fleshly things. If you're walking in the Spirit, it's because you put your mind on spiritual things.

Imagine a truck filled with concrete. The concrete is eventually going to take the shape of whatever mold it's poured into—a driveway, a patio, a retaining wall, a road, or a foundation. The concrete cannot take any form unless a mold is created. Your thoughts are like the mold. Your thoughts create a shape for God to pour His power into, to do something with your life. If you want a powerful life, choose to keep your mind on things that agree with God's will so He can work with you toward your goals.

Power Thought: My mind is set on spiritual things.

About the Author

JOYCE MEYER is one of the world's leading practical Bible teachers. A #1 *New York Times* bestselling author, she has written nearly 100 inspirational books, including *Change Your Words, Change Your Life, Making Good Habits, Breaking Bad Habits*, the entire Battlefield of the Mind family of books, and two novels, *The Penny* and *Any Minute*, as well as many others. She has also released thousands of audio teachings, as well as a complete video library. Joyce's *Enjoying Everyday Life*® radio and television programs are broadcast around the world, and she travels extensively conducting conferences. Joyce and her husband, Dave, are the parents of four grown children and make their home in St. Louis, Missouri.

Other Books by Joyce Meyer

100 Ways to Simplify Your Life
The Secret to True Happiness
Reduce Me to Love
The Secret Power of Speaking God's Word

Devotionals

Love Out Loud Devotional
The Confident Woman Devotional
Hearing from God Each Morning
New Day, New You Devotional
Battlefield of the Mind Devotional
Ending Your Day Right*
Starting Your Day Right*

* Also available in Spanish